Roots of Musicality

of related interest

Music Therapy – Intimate Notes
Mercédès Pavlicevic
ISBN 1 85302 692 1

Music, Music Therapy and Trauma
International Perspectives
Edited by Julie P. Sutton
ISBN 1 84310 027 4

Community Music Therapy
Edited by Mercédès Pavlicevic and Gary Ansdell
Foreword by Even Ruud
ISBN 1 84310 124 6

Health, the Individual, and Integrated Medicine
Revisiting an Aesthetic of Health Care
David Aldridge
ISBN 1 84310 232 3

Music Therapy, Sensory Integration and the Autistic Child
Dorita S. Berger
Foreword by Donna Williams
ISBN 1 84310 700 7

Music Therapy in Children's Hospices
Celebrating Jessie's Fund
Edited by Mercédès Pavlicevic
Foreword by Victoria Wood
ISBN 1 84310 254 4

Music Therapy in Neurological Health Care Settings
Performing Health
Edited by David Aldridge
ISBN 1 84310 302 8

Roots of Musicality
Music Therapy and Personal Development

Daniel Perret

Foreword by Colwyn Trevarthen

Jessica Kingsley Publishers
London and Philadelphia

Sounding bowl shown on front cover by Tobias Kaye.

Photograph on p.156 by Raphael Duss. Photograph on p.157 by Sabina Gränicher. Photograph on p.158 by PANArt.

Table on p.177–181 adapted from *Improvisational Models of Music Therapy* by Kenneth Bruscia, reproduced with the permission of Charles C. Thomas.

Extracts on pp.163–4 from Dorit Amir's article 'Research in Music Therapy: Quantitative or Qualitative?' (1993), published in the *Nordic Journal of Music Therapy 2*, 2, reproduced with the permission of the *Nordic Journal of Music Therapy*. The poems on p.49 and p.87 and the excerpts from a poem and a short story on pp.15, 25 and 137 are reproduced with the kind permission of the author, Marie Perret.

First published in French in 2004 by Souffle d'Or as *Evoluer par la musique et les 5 éléments*

First published in English in 2005
by Jessica Kingsley Publishers
116 Pentonville Road
London N1 9JB, UK
and
400 Market Street, Suite 400
Philadelphia, PA 19106, USA

www.jkp.com

Library of Congress Cataloging in Publication Data

Perret, Daniel Gilbert, 1950
    [Evoluer par la musique et les 5 elements. English]
    Roots of musicality : music therapy and personal development / Daniel Perret ; foreword by Colwyn Trevarthen.-- 1st American pbk. ed.
        p. cm.
    Translation of: Evoluer par la musique et les 5 elements.
    Includes bibliographical references (p.   ) and indexes.
    ISBN-13: 978-1-84310-336-3 (pbk.)
    ISBN-10: 1-84310-336-2 (pbk.)

    1. Music therapy. 2. Music--Psychological aspects. 3. Music, Influence of. I. Title.
    ML3920.P342 2005
    781'.11--dc22

                    2004026199

British Library Cataloguing in Publication Data
A CIP catalogue record for this book is available from the British Library

ISBN-13: 978 1 84310 336 3
ISBN-10: 1 84310 336 2

Printed and Bound in Great Britain by
Athenaeum Press, Gateshead, Tyne and Wear

Contents

Foreword
Finding New Energy for Life
in Music Shared

This is a book about music and the human spirit. It attempts to explain how the spirit of a child may be enlivened by music. Daniel Perret is a musician who plays in dialogue with young minds and bodies to liberate them from restraint and isolation. He uses a map of the field of human energies to guide him. His task is often difficult. Finding a way forward, around barriers, may take patience. There is always a chance, however, that the music will spark the fire of life and creativity, setting a spirit free and bringing happiness. Music, being part of the source of life always changes us, in small or tremendous ways. It colours and fixes our memories. It gives narrative strength to our experiences and to the recollections of life. It enters into the body, moving and exciting, feeding vitality. In skilled and sympathetic hands, it can educate and heal.

Daniel's interest in energy fields draws attention to the sensations of movement within hidden parts of the body, as well as to the mastery of the environment of objects and space outside. It asks us to take generous interest in unfamiliar explanations of the body as a place of life where music can find an effective echo. Our ignorance of what it is that happens to us when we are enthralled by the narratives of music should advise us to suspend disbelief and to listen to how Daniel applies his metaphors to strengthen the work he does as a music therapist.

I understand 'musicality' to be a product of our unique human way of acting in and sensing the world (Trevarthen 1999), of being conscious of meaning through collective 'mimesis' (Donald 2001). All agile creatures have to master their movements by linking inner and outer organs. They must conduct the mechanics of trunk and limbs, overcoming their mass and inertia to rise from the surface of the earth and swim, fly or run. They do so with pulses of muscular effort, estimating the future of their progression in measures of time, and tracking their displacements in a space with its centre of reference in the body. All prospective benefits and costs of 'animacy', the movement of the 'soul', are planned in images to be lived. Each navigating organism must also hold intact and regulate the secret movements of internal organs, planning essential vitality with due regard for fatigue, pain and pleasure. All expense of mechanical energy in moving has to be sensed in accord with the physiological/chemical energy in the processes of living cells. Each self is a dynamic project incorporating many components.

When the spirit is engaged, it is the whole self who responds – identity, imagination and memories, thoughts, relationships and bodily well-being. Dynamic events that sustain and energise life are carried in the sound of body movement, for which the different dynamic properties of earth, air, metal, fire and water are like tools that we can master to celebrate experience.

The sound of music penetrates the whole of our being. It not only stirs our heavy muscled skeletons. It also resonates in our 'heart', exciting or pacifying. It may make us tense and scared, thrill us or carry us to peace and rest. It may lift us from the present bringing to mind remote places or persons, reconstructing events. The spirit that answers to music is in the activity of both soma and viscera. It changes both the substance and quality of experience by engaging with the motives that regulate our life.

Musical art is the sound of the body moving made 'special' as a message (Dissanayake 1999). In any piece of music, however composed or played, we hear light stepping feet, heavy swaying hips, gestures with graceful arms and nimble fingers, their rhythms syncopated. We hear hitting, stroking and plucking of objects with affecting resonance and timbre. Music also projects voice sounds from inside the body, carrying signs of the visceral joy of affection, of calm pleasure, of painful tension and of violent anger. It describes all the levels of the body's movement – the pulse of stepping feet that run, walk, trip and dance, mastering the earth; the rhythmic swing of hips and belly that glide and sway with dignity, light grace or flirtatious impudence. It can stimulate enfeebling pain of anxiety in the belly or the burning ardour of the breast and the alert intelligence of the head and eyes and lips, those parts that can break free with a versatility of invention that leaves the heavy limbs behind, telling metaphors for imagined worlds and activities in other times and places, abstracting symbols and putting them into words.

Music reports the endless variations of gesture that flow from shoulders to agile fingers, setting the two hands complementary tasks in the narrative of sound. By fingering responsive instruments a musician imitates the speed and intricate sequences of speech in a realm of expression that leaves the heavy body behind, describing thoughts, memories and dreams that can take place anywhere at any time – in the intellect of the head. But no thoughts are free of the vital embodied rule of emotion. Even the most artificial symbolic code carries emotive associations in its metaphors, old memories that can inspire or breed confusion and despair.

Musical art can also project the vitality of the human body empathically onto events in the animate and inanimate non-human world. It can imitate the actions and mood of beasts, and it can create illusions of space, of objects in motion and of climatic storms or oceans of sunny serenity. We animate from the spirit everything we conceive, and our art takes on the forms of energy in all experience.

Of course I am drawing parallels with Daniel's five elements, with the different dynamic properties of earth, air, fire and water. I recognise the power of these ancient metaphors, but prefer to take them back to the life of the body. I see that the diagram of energy fields and the seven centres portrays a sexless, angel-like body of a lone person, eyes and mouth closed, with arms held down in a diagram of inactivity. I want the musical energy to be seen as a body that dances and sings by moving all its parts, rising in the space of imagination and companionship, making melodies of expression that invite engagement and offer energy or rest. I repeat, music is the sound of the body *moving*, even when it portrays a centred calm that makes us still.

Daniel mentions the brain and the new science of emotions in cognition. We are all watching to see what new inventions can teach us about what goes on in our heads when we think and feel and intend to move in different ways, and when we respond to one another (Adolphs 2003; Decety and Chaminade 2003). Science makes slow progress towards a richer awareness of motivation – the values of the spirit that enliven the body and mind. It finds checks and balances of motive at many levels, conscious and unconscious, that economise and expend the energy of life.

Cognitive brain science has difficulty grappling with the visceral economy that rules at a subconscious level, that determines our sense of

well-being or distress, of vigour or fatigue and that communicates appre-
hensive emotions that anticipate joy or fears suffering in our social relationships (Panksepp 2000). What we do know tells us that the expressive
intelligence of interest signalled by the eyes and the way the lips and
voice convey changing pleasure and displeasure in interpersonal life,
giving moral values to relationships and to our selves have evolved from
systems that regulate breath, the flow of the blood and feeding and
digestion. Excitements and feelings of well-being or ill health are manifestations of control for the metabolism of life – for the vital energy
economy of tissues and organs hidden within us. This understanding
helps explain why music can so deeply affect our sense of vitality and
health, and how it can be used in therapy (Trevarthen and Malloch 2000;
Panksepp and Bernatzky 2002).

The fact that consciousness is different in the left and right hemispheres of the brain is puzzling and fascinating, and it is certainly
important for understanding emotional pathology (Schore 2003). The
cerebral hemispheres seem like brother and sister in consciousness and
emotion, with subtly different intelligences and personalities, and the
right is perhaps more emotional, musical and feminine, and it develops
more quickly before language is acquired. There are, however, many
paradoxes.

The story neuropsychology tells is surely a very provisional one. For
example, a left-handed female child is likely to speak early and may be a
willing and able singer. Left-handed males rarely have these talents, but
they may have special visuo-spatial interests. Where does this leave the
idea that the left hemisphere is male and the right female? I think that the
evidence is that the cognitive and 'executive' (thought organising) differences found by psychologists with their intelligence tests in left and right
sides of the cerebral cortex reflect a deeper, and more ancient, left–right
asymmetry of motives. These motives either command the body to act
boldly on the world with intricate goal-directed motor sequences,
chancing that there will be enough energy, or seek to conserve resources
of the self and its body by holding a wider view of circumstances, and by
sympathetic response to other sensitive selves.

All the evidence available points to an intricate and variable
complementarity between patches of tissue in different lobes of the
cortex, all of which are but foliage of different colours on the canopy of a

forest of neural systems whose roots are far below, often out of reach of functional brain imaging. Moreover, the brain's processing of the information by which actions are planned and guided is so fast that our recording tools can rarely catch more than a blur of what is happening. I judge that brain science is far from leading to the explanation of natural musicality. I doubt if it offers much to explain the work of Daniel as a music therapist. In this he and I tend to agree.

Perhaps the most remarkable discovery of psychological research into the origins of human nature in recent time is that an infant is born not only sensitive to the musicality of another person's expressions, but capable of moving with the music of movements, imitating and questioning the melody, sympathetic for the energy in it (Trehub 1999; Trevarthen and Malloch 2002). Babies are alert to the pulse, quality and narrative of a mother's talk and song (Malloch 1999). They appreciate beauty in musical sound and move in time with it. They are distressed by discord or lack of 'attunement' in another's expressions, sensing detachment as alienation (Stern 1999). Following the development of musicality in the games of infants and parents we see how this active celebration of enjoyment in shared activity is serious preparation for learning what others know and do. It is in the structure of the bridge between understandings of teacher and learner, and it helps the adult meet what the child is discovering as they cross this bridge together.

I value this book mainly for the evidence it brings from the author's experience of making contact with autistic children, and from sharing their fears and hopes. The way Daniel traces the evolution of a child's motives to meet with them and to invite a contribution to a musical game or dialogue opens up a wealth of topics which I think are of crucial importance, not only for therapy with children who are so defensive and inarticulate, but for all our understanding of the development and growth of the human spirit.

I am convinced that there are thresholds of energy that a child or a relationship may need to surmount. Indeed, any person adventuring into new experiences must encounter them. Entering a new level of expressiveness and awareness of the possibilities of life entails risk and demands concentration. It has to be planned. Readiness to move forward often comes suddenly, as a release.

> We have seen that in normal development of an infant there are regressive periods followed by advances in competence and understanding. Indeed, we have described infancy as a succession of age-related Periods of Rapid Change. Most famously, there is the great transformation, which some call a 'revolution', that occurs around 9 months after birth when a child senses the goals of others and seeks, for the first time, to cooperate or engage with their purposes, accepting the new ideas and values involved. (Trevarthen and Aitken 2003)

This we describe as a threshold to an understanding of other's meanings, and to catching the sense of words.

Therapists have found the account of 'transitions' in normal infancy of value in explaining sudden advances in interest, skill and communication observed in a client's responses, and their active contributions to joint enjoyment of the creative task. It is like the removal of a blockage, the opening of clouds. I believe that the cause of these 'discontinuous' events in human achievement must be understood as products of the motivating process, the dynamic system that regulates life's energy resources.

Actions require prediction, of the risks and potential benefits of committing the body that way. The state of the spirit determines what may be imagined with confidence – what future the self has. A traumatised child or one whose development has not created the confident awareness that meets the needs of certain tasks, will either not attain the level of anticipation that can make action possible, or will block it, protectively.

We expect a child to reach out toward us playfully, adventurously, exuberantly, affectionately, knowing we will share fun and help with difficulties. An autistic child is puzzlingly unwilling in some respects, and too focused on other private needs for us to comprehend. That is why, as with any child who has a handicap in acting and relating, a parent, therapist or teacher has to sensitively find the place 'where the child is', and imagine his or her world, with its gaps and fears.

As Daniel shows us, you have to 'reach out' and be alert for any sign of approach or an opening of the spirit for sharing play and invention. Music offered in this responsive way, is often the key that frees the child's enjoyment and creativity. We must pay attention to Daniel's explanations of how he has found that key for a child and opened the door to action in sound they could enjoy together.

Colwyn Trevarthen
Professor of Neurobiology, The University of Edinburgh

References

Adolphs, R. (2003) 'Investigating the cognitive neuroscience of social behavior.' *Neuropsychologia 41*, 119–126.

Decety, J. and Chaminade, T. (2003) 'Neural correlates of feeling sympathy.' *Neuropsychologia 41*, 127–138.

Dissanayake, E. (1999) 'Antecedents of the temporal arts in early mother–infant interaction.' In N. Wallin and B. Merker (eds) *The Origins of Music*. Cambridge, MA: MIT Press.

Donald, M. (2001) *A Mind So Rare: The Evolution of Human Consciousness*. New York and London: Norton.

Malloch, S. (1999) 'Mothers and infants and communicative musicality.' In *Rhythms, Musical Narrative, and the Origins of Human Communication. Musicae Scientiae, Special Issue, 1999–2000*, 29–57. Liège: European Society for the Cognitive Sciences of Music.

Panksepp, J. (2000) 'The neuro-evolutionary cusp between emotions and cognitions, implications for understand consciousness and the emergence of a unified mind science.' *Consciousness and Emotion 1*, 17–56.

Panksepp, J. and Bernatzky, G. (2002) 'Emotional sounds and the brain: The neuro-affective foundations of musical appreciation.' *Behavioural Processes 60*, 133–155.

Schore, A.N. (2003) *Affect Regulation and Disorders of the Self*. New York: Norton.

Stern, D.N. (1999) 'Vitality contours: the temporal contour of feelings as a basic unit for constructing the infant's social experience.' In P. Rochat (ed) *Early Social Cognition: Understanding Others in the First Months of Life*. Mahwah, NJ: Erlbaum.

Trehub, S.E. (1990) 'The perception of musical patterns by human infants: The provision of similar patterns by their parents.' In M.A. Berkley and W.C. Stebbins (eds) *Comparative Perception; Vol. 1, Mechanisms*. New York: Wiley.

Trevarthen, C. (1999) 'Musicality and the Intrinsic Motive Pulse: Evidence from human psychobiology and infant communication.' In *Rhythms, Musical Narrative, and the Origins of Human Communication. Musicae Scientiae, Special Issue, 1999–2000*, 157–213. Liège: European Society for the Cognitive Sciences of Music.

Trevarthen, C. and Aitken, K.J. (2003) 'Regulation of brain development and age-related changes in infants' motives: The developmental function of "regressive" periods.' In M. Heimann (ed) *Regression Periods in Human Infancy*. Mahwah, NJ: Erlbaum.

Trevarthen, C. and Malloch, S. (2000) 'The dance of wellbeing: Defining the musical therapeutic effect.' *Nordic Journal of Music Therapy 9*, 2, 3–17.

Trevarthen, C. and Malloch, S. (2002) 'Musicality and music before three: Human vitality and invention shared with pride.' *Zero to Three 23*, 1, 10–18.

Rhythm of Life (excerpt)

There are times when my focus shifts
deeper than what I am seeing,
like falling into an underlying current
behind the physical world of appearances
where everything is colour, movements, and sound
an interweaving, vibrating pulsation that flows
into birth, through life, through death.
It never stops, there's never a break…

Marie Perret, 1999

Introduction

I am fascinated both as a musician and as a music therapist by the fact that the word 'harmony' is a musical term as well as a word used in daily life. Very often the word is used without understanding why the same word pertains to music and to life in general.

We talk readily about harmony in a couple, in a family, in a village or in a commercial organisation. We talk about 'living in harmony with…'. But once harmony is lost, what can we actually do to restore it? What exactly is missing? Which ingredient? Is it a particular state of mind that has vanished? Which one would that be?

Neuroscientists have observed and documented that humans are born with an innate musicality which is expressed in the very earliest exchanges with our parents. Researchers using audio and video recordings and computer analysis, have found that in the communications between parents and toddlers there are rhythms, musical bars, melody, nuances in intonation, in fact all the ingredients that make music. Even when we are babies we cannot but be musical. All our communication is coloured by the rhythms of our brain, our heart, our breathing and our digestion. Our communications dance through the expression of our emotions and feelings from the tiniest movement by the baby's fingers, to its face, arms and legs. Even our physical anatomy, the fact of having two legs for instance, enhances our natural propensity for rhythms of two or four beats per bar, whereas the rest of the body, the independent movements of our arms, hands, head and our heartbeat, engage us naturally in polyrhythms, multiple and simultaneous rhythms. We experienced these rhythms previously in the womb, a universe mainly made up of sounds and tastes. We can call this our *biological musicality*.

The relatively new discipline of bioacoustics, partially inspired by Tomatis' work in France, is trying to prove that each muscle, each organ or part of our skeleton, produces its own sound, a frequency. This makes of us a bit of a symphony. Our *inborn musicality*, though, goes beyond this purely biological aspect. There is the memory of what we heard in our mother's womb, her voice, her heartbeat as well as our own, the voices of other family members, the noises of her digestion, of the environment, songs or music. Most of the time there would be a feeling or emotion associated with such experiences of sound. All these sounds stem either directly from our mother or come from elsewhere outside and are filtered by her, by her body and her whole being, and include her own emotional reactions to any 'sound' event in the outside environment.

Of course there is also a *cultural musicality* present in the larger environment in which we have grown up. This musicality will depend on our parents' taste in music, the presence or absence of music at school, our musical education, the music to which we have listened on the radio, on records, at concerts, on the television and at the cinema, for example. This multiple sound environment has inevitably transmitted to us a vast musical memory. Our etheric energy field may store every single piece of sensory information. For a while I worked with a boy in music therapy whose mother came from Cameroon. There was no doubt that he had been exposed to a wealth of rhythms that are not common in our western culture. These cultural transmissions would have started in the womb and would come not only from acoustic sounds but very likely would also be received through the mother's subconscious, her etheric energy field. I know from personal experience that we can also draw on sound experiences from past lives.

Stephen Malloch, an Australian musician and scientist, talks of 'communicative musicality' present from the first weeks of our lives (Trevarthen and Malloch 2000). The neurobiologist Colwyn Trevarthen underlines this:

> The new-born has an innate appreciation of the dynamics of emotions that inhabit the human movements and specially their expression through the voice, combined with an awareness of the evolution of the 'emotional narrative' – expressing the changing qualities of feelings that follow cycles or slow waves of excitement and vitality...

When a mother sings a children's song, the baby joins in with her and participates in moving his fingers and arms, smiling happily, uttering some sounds that often anticipate and underline the end of a phrase. The rhythm that underlies any mother–baby conversation allows the child to anticipate events in the narrative. The whole becomes an intimate 'dance' between two participants that becomes visible when one films and compares the simultaneous expressions on their faces.

Beyond a biological musicality, an innate cultural musicality and a learned musicality which is strengthened through the rituals in our first weeks of life that bring about the first unfolding of language, there are most likely to be at least two more dimensions of musicality that I feel are sufficiently important to be taken into consideration. Both dimensions relate to energy. One is the *empathetic capacity* of our energy field, and more particularly of the thyroid chakra, which is linked to hearing and expression. The second is associated with what many call a universal or spiritual source. Musicality is also an expression that allows us, through the sensitivity of our thyroid chakra which surpasses our five physical senses, to follow all movements of expression on a very subtle and intimate level. This can be observed when we are listening carefully to someone speaking. In this situation we may catch ourselves, or others, moving their lips in synchronicity with the speaker. We may feel in our own bodies the movements the speaker makes with his head, his fingers or his arms, for example. Colwyn Trevarthen reports from his personal observations the same phenomenon that neuroscientists have found in one part of the brain. This brain centre allows someone to register and reproduce simultaneously the movements seen in another person.

This research documents a very sophisticated empathetic quality that allows us to identify with the other's expression, even on a feeling level, as if we were inside his skin. This faculty allows us to develop a musicality that integrates the processes of mind together with transpersonal dimensions such as inspirations from unknown sources and to communicate them. We find ourselves face to face with the foundations of our cultural expression. These give us the means with which we may participate intimately in visions; we may express and transmit them. It enables us to elaborate concepts and to translate intuitions of feelings which spoken language cannot adequately express.

Musicality is also the expression of a sense of harmony, of beauty, of balance and respect. These are for me *universal* or *spiritual qualities*. If this musicality is partly of a biological nature present during the first months of our lives, it becomes over time the expression of our emotions, feelings and is possibly a reflection of our spiritual qualities. Our innate musicality becomes greatly enlarged and is transformed through our wish to grow, through our thirst for harmony. When we express ourselves musically in a spontaneous way we always communicate 'something' which is most likely to be feelings in our inner self, or sometimes impulses coming from a level beyond our personality. This can happen when singing, moving and dancing, when playing an instrument, be it an improvisation, while composing, during a music lesson, while making music with friends, at a concert, in a therapeutic situation, or when playing as an amateur or professional musician.

In order to understand certain dimensions present in therapeutic work and in personal development, we need to have a wider vision, we need a *cosmogony*. This implies that we need to have an understanding of the All-There-Is, to ask ourselves questions about how we participate in global harmony, to see how closely our own destiny is linked with the well-being of the planet, of people near and far and with the heavenly rhythms, with the elements in nature. Harmony cannot be established partially. The events in the world remind us of this. We are all concerned by the exploitation and humiliation of individuals, people and nature. People and the elements seem always to find ways to remind us, they rebel. Suicide attacks are a desperate means of expression, even if they are often not perceived as such and contribute to further desperation. Nature manifests itself through earthquakes and recently with spectacular floods, forest fires, storms and tornadoes as well as periods of extreme drought.

My approach to the Ancient Greek and Indian *five elements system*: *earth, water, fire, air* and *space*, enables us to understand the link between nature, quality in musical expression and the inner roots of our musicality. This system links us with the whole of nature, with the animal world as well as with its invisible aspects and allows us to distinguish criteria of felt quality. I call this level *shamanic*. I shall also be using a *tantric* level of inner energy awareness. I shall write about this later on.

We know when a piece of music is not harmonious and when an orchestra is not performing harmoniously. We can of course tune a musical instrument. But even with this correct tuning it is sometimes quite difficult to put one's finger on what exactly is wrong and dis-harmonious, what or who in a deeper sense is not 'in tune'. If we discuss this we would sooner or later have to talk about 'musicality', that is the sensitivity of a musician to 'get in tune' and to know how to create harmony by selectively changing this or that musical element: speed, phrasing, key and mode come to mind. We would again find ourselves confronting what we might call a 'state of mind'. Musicality is very likely the reflection of what we are about to feel within ourselves, what we are about to become, what is emerging, as if musical expression was a 'fingerprint' of the one who plays or sings. A fingerprint that would be unique and involuntary.

Let us settle on some definitions of terms I use in this book. *Musicality* is considered to be the ability to handle the qualitative aspects of musical communication, in the sense that beyond the use of conventional musical language it expresses the underlying levels of our spirit, of our innermost self. *Harmony* describes the momentary balance between the elements of a system. This system can be a piece of music, a person, a couple, a group of people or indeed a whole ecological system. When I use the word *creativity* I am thinking of the natural creative life force in of each us that expresses itself through us, suggesting in a continuous natural flow new solutions and visions. The sources of creativity can stem from all kinds of levels, from the emotional to the spiritual. When I use the word *musician* I include all amateurs, all those looking for a kind of magic, something that fascinates them about singing alone or in a choir, playing any instrument from a simple singing bowl to the most sophisticated.

Practising music is practising and learning how to bring about harmony. This practice is very much linked to our state of mind, our capacity to grasp globally or intuitively the complexity of the elements participating in establishing harmony and to learn how to respect them better. I believe firmly that the word 'harmony' is not by chance used in music as in life.

I shall be describing what I consider to be *bridges between music and life*, demonstrating that both are ultimately the expression of the same phenomena, namely energy and spirit. This leads us to understand that by listening to a person playing or singing or when we watch someone dancing we can see right through the performer, seeing her as a psycho-energetic system serving a soul purpose, expressing spirit. I have written mostly about practising live music, not so much about recorded music. I did that extensively in my previous book (Perret 1997).

Many musicians, composers and therapists feel the need to create beneficial or healing sound spaces and want to know how to generate harmony and magic, they want to understand what the roots of musicality are. The question of meaning arises with insistence.

I write last but not least for the amateur musicians, who listen to music but who also love to *play* on an instrument in a playful sense of the word. We will see that through a voice, a singing bowl or a simple hand drum one can express the essence of music. What I aim at is a depth of feeling and not technical skills. I feel very strongly in all that I do in music, about encouraging the *playful* use of any musical instrument. If someone is to open up to his creativity, his playful side and the experimental, then he needs courage to approach new horizons, to meet the unknown. Musical expression is everyone's birthright and in this search for meaning is it necessary to emphasise that no musical genre is better than any other. As far as I am concerned it is about the depth of feeling expressed.

New approaches are required because numerous people do not find what they need in the conventional way music is taught in the west. Fundamentally music touches our hearts, it unites heaven and earth in us, it awakens our aspirations and our deepest needs and because all this is happening in the heart we suffer when we do not find in music what we are searching for deep within us. To have contact with harmony inevitably highlights the disharmonies in our lives more vividly and painfully. When these roles of music are denied, musicians, whether students, amateurs or even professionals, sooner or later experience feelings of despair. They can feel that the 'source' is close by and yet at the same time they become ever more aware of its distance. The feeling approach to music is absolutely essential (Perret 1997). The current time makes us painfully aware of this. If harmony is not understood in its natural musical world, it will be difficult to re-establish it in any other field such as in the environment, in families, in schools, at work and in philosophical studies (Biesenbender 2001).

When we are teaching music we should remember that score reading, the technical aspect of playing an instrument, the history of music, the birth and death dates of a composer, even recalling their names are all disciplines of the left side of the brain, the intellect. The essence of music is not there, music moves our hearts.

Having observed for more than twenty years what is happening when sound and music are used as healing tools, it is evident that we are living in a fascinating time full of discoveries. The same is true for the sciences of the brain. I note, though, a void between the world of music therapists and the research being done by others on the effects of sound. I do not think that this serves any good purpose. It is in my nature to look for bridges and to encourage synthesis everywhere. I was happy to read the excellent article by Dorit Amir (1993) in the *Nordic Journal of Music Therapy* on the necessity to make qualitative research in music therapy. She explains how the old axioms in research have to be replaced by new paradigms (see Appendix 2).

I want to share something exciting that I have been observing for a number of years now, *neuro-musical thresholds.* These are phenomena of significant changes in a person's behaviour that seem to be triggered by working on specific musical tasks that he or she appears to be resisting. The tasks are 'easy' ones, there is no logical explanation for experiencing them as difficult and yet one can sometimes work with patients for weeks and months on the same task. The long-lasting difficulties experienced by some patients before crossing them has lead me to label them 'thresholds'. My observations stem partly from my work with adults but a large part of my work has been with young children at the Centre d'Accueil Thérapeutique à Temps Partiel (CATTP) – a day clinic in Brive Hospital, Central France.

We have been taught and have become accustomed to consider as scientific all work done mainly with the left side of the brain, that is work based on analytical, logical, measurable, visible and material criteria. This attitude is not in itself scientific. In fact it is rather medieval and doctrinaire. It excludes anything contributed by the right side of the brain such as intuition, feeling, energy and spiritual elements. New questions demand new tools. This is what gave birth to the invention of the microscope and thereafter previously invisible things suddenly became visible and consequently became a part of science.

I am used to working with both sides of the brain, combining feeling and intuition with the analytical. It works well. One can proceed to do this in several stages. I start with a clear mental conception of what I want to focus on, left brain action. I observe the object of focus first with the left then with the right side of the brain, maybe using some memorising tools such as spontaneous drawing. I analyse the observations and finish by combining both hemispheres of the brain to deepen the understanding of what has been observed and to reach conclusions. The combined use of both sides of the brain takes a bit of practice, as does the use of a microscope. Quantum physics has tried to make us aware of this duality since the middle of the last century. We are matter *and* energy. It is time to take this in. As a good friend of mine brought to us:

The mind – like the parachute – works best when open.

I have had the opportunity to meet two great masters in musical matters, both were Irish. Willie Reynolds from near Athlone taught me to play the Irish uilleann pipes, together with all the ways of being so much a part of that musical tradition, which is to say generosity, humility and respect for the richness and precision of oral transmission (Willie Reynolds 1990).

Robert (Bob) Moore taught me for twenty years in a scientific way how to study the human energy fields through observation. He used a lot of recorded music in his teachings, having us observe on a subtle level what the sounds did in and around us. He had the understanding to use a precise recording after a specific energy awareness exercise in order to enhance the effects of the exercise. I dedicate this book to them.

I had the good luck to have an uncle and aunt in Brittany, both working in the medical profession. In my youth I had many happy holidays in their home – times that created a fortunate association between nature, happiness, medicine and Celtic music. My deep connection with the Celtic Culture in Ireland, Brittany and in Scotland where I studied the highland pipes, and in Switzerland too where I was born (Switzerland being the Helvetic Confederation, the Helvetes were a Celtic tribe just as much as the Celts who lived in Perigord in South-West France where I live now with my family) is one strong source of inspiration for me. The other is the meditative culture developed in the Far East, the Zen part in me, that is also very present in my music albums.

Music has always reminded me of my true 'home'. The sounds of the bagpipes for instance or of a distant flute have this effect on me. I have always felt that certain musical experiences and the impact they have on us could heal us in the sense of enabling us to feel whole again.

Working with the five elements system and neuro-musical thresholds allows us to understand the links between musical expression and inner phenomena of a psycho-energetic nature. These ways of working can become valuable tools in music teaching, healing and music therapy. Each obstacle in musical expression reveals its cause. It becomes knowable. A lack of musicality can be linked to what happens in specific areas of our body, to associated thought structures, emotions and beliefs. All these connections can be used as keys to develop our musicality, to understand the reason for a specific disharmony and to give us concrete ways of working. Musical harmony becomes the harmony of the whole being. The veil is lifting.

Rhythm of Life (excerpt)

…Each being is part of this vast tapestry of creation –
a vibration of intense and vivid colour and sound.
The laws of life are shaping these movements.
We are each a colour, a vibration, a sound
and we constantly modify this through our thoughts.
We create ourselves and our life experiences from within.
This whole movement is very precise and scientific.
It is not on an emotional level,
it is held in a vast expanse of silence
and all living human and animal experience
is within this…

Marie Perret, 1999

Chapter 1

The Psycho-energetic
Approach to Music

Observing energy

The psycho-energetic approach to music has the following principal characteristics:

- the spiritual dimension
- the human energy fields
- the key role of our inborn qualities.

In addition, I have a particular interest in researching not only the effects on people when they hear musical instruments and other sounds but also their therapeutic uses. Finally, I believe that consciousness and its development, together with intuition, play a key role in all of this. This is why I teach and suggest awareness exercises to further personal development.

The word *psycho-energetic* brings to mind the effort that must be made to observe the effects of sounds on our psyche, that is to say on our thoughts, imagination, emotions and feelings, as well as on the energy fields found within and beyond the physical body. This word refers to the whole psychosomatic dimension as well as to the spiritual level, a level that is mainly energetic and hence virtually non-physical. In my understanding, though, there is no significant separation between the spiritual and the physical. I emphasise the importance of a psycho-energetic approach, in contrast to acoustic, musicological, physical or psychological approaches. In so doing I am underlining the importance of consciousness, that is the combination of our conscious feelings and thoughts as well as the effects of sound on all observable levels. Without this combination of sound and consciousness I maintain that all musical activities in therapy or self development would be of only temporary benefit, thus not very useful in the longer term.

I use the word *emotion* for painful phenomena in the lower astral field. Among these are hatred, anger, insecurity, fear, jealousy, despair and depression. I use the word *feelings* to describe non-painful states in the astral energy field (the emotional part of the aura), often called the upper astral. Among these are love, compassion, a sense of beauty, serenity and joy. The astral is one of the energy fields that make up our psycho-energetic system. The other energy fields being the etheric, the mental and the spiritual aura.

Inborn spiritual qualities: the key

Our inborn spiritual qualities are the key to deeper healing processes. In many western countries people have quite an ambiguous attitude towards spirituality. The proponents of church doctrines have for a long time had an almost total monopoly on the subject. The decline of the church's authority went hand in hand with the separation of state and church and of school and church. This has left many people disoriented and in a void as far as spiritual matters are concerned. It is common nowadays that many people no longer know what to think about anything connected with spirituality. Often people may automatically reject anything even remotely connected to it, because they immediately associate spiritual concerns with a dominating and suffocating authority, or with divisive sectarian or occult movements. Along with this attitude there is an exaggerated scepticism towards anything seen falsely to be 'irrational' and therefore incapable of being categorised, labelled, analysed or measured by the techniques developed by mankind mainly in the brain's left hemisphere. This is what we call somewhat casually 'the cartesian spirit' while conveniently forgetting that Descartes' thinking went a long way beyond the purely intellectual or rational.

However, we must realise that this spiritual void in western culture has given rise to considerable anxiety and suffering. The ever-rising consumption of drugs, medical and non-medical, and other mind alterers may be one eloquent witness to the spiritual void experienced by so many of us. This lack of spiritual orientation has tragic results not least in the therapeutic field. For when a human being cannot sense his place in the global or universal context, he will lack a sense of orientation and will find it very difficult to grasp essential wisdom and attain inner peace. It is fortunate for us that nowadays there are a number of quality teachings accessible to anyone who is looking for enduring answers. But since there are few if no reliable external authorities who can guarantee the value of any chosen path, we have no other choice than to discriminate and learn for ourselves how to distinguish the authentic from the fake in the spiritual as well as in the material spheres.

I think that it is necessary when considering music and its effects to ask oneself some fundamental questions and to build up one's own beliefs concerning life, spirituality, consciousness, energy, intuition, inspiration, the meaning of life and death, what may come before our physical lives and after our death, creativity, our inborn qualities and from where they come.

The psycho-energetic approach differs from a purely psychological one in giving an important role to the spiritual dimension. Our contact with our qualities plays a key role in all of this and will ensure that we do not get lost in childhood traumas and the inevitable sufferings of life in general. Personally I am convinced that the only way to resist the force of suffering is ultimately to give it less importance, which means that we must strengthen the spiritual aspects of our existence. Contacting our spiritual dimension gives us a different perspective on our personal history and allows us to distance ourselves somewhat from our suffering. Spirituality furnishes us with a vision, an overview and strengthens us. Very often we cannot solve our problems by storming head-on into them. The more we fight with them, the more we give them significance and energy. This is where I agree with Buddhist teachings and with the point of view of French psychotherapist François Roustang, as he describes it in his book *La Fin de la Plainte* [*An End to Complaining*] (2000).

When we stop complaining the whole therapeutic attitude changes completely.

> 'Feather' had long curly red hair. She often was in a bad mood and used to take everybody by surprise with her lightning fast movements. Someone would get a kick in the leg or struck by some spit before anyone noticed what she was about to do. Her family situation did not help her behaviour either. I had thought at first to

take her into music therapy with another child. I had to stop doing that very soon after I had started it because she needed my whole attention. Playing music was not at all her favourite activity, but she did very much like to come to music therapy. At first she would often be depressive and crouch next to the door or in a corner of the room. Then she moved into a phase where she continuously wanted to climb on my back or sit on my knees. What struck me very early on was how she would dance with completely stiff legs as if she had no knees at all.

Like many children who come to our day clinic she had severe language problems. We had to guess almost everything she tried to communicate. By and by, after some three months in music therapy she tried to make me understand that she would like to dance. She held up her arms towards me and insisted on me lifting her by the arms and making her jump in the air. She wanted to put little bell bracelets on her ankles. I guessed that the sound of the bells was helping her to bring her energy down to her feet so as to improve her sense of grounding each time she did a step or jumped. I lifted her repeatedly to make her jump until my arms were aching. But every time I stopped she would start screaming.

This ritual went on for weeks and I was trying desperately to find a way out of it and to bring about some kind of development. Luckily I had the idea of singing a rhythmical song while she was jumping. After doing this for a while I would let go of her arms for a few seconds while still dancing and singing with her and clapping our hands together at the same time. She fortunately chose to copy me. Then I would pick up her arms again. The next time I let go we managed to turn around on ourselves before I grabbed her arms again. She enjoyed that too, clapping her hands all the while. Finally we managed to dance around the large frame drum that I had placed in the middle of the floor. That is when the 'miracle' happened. She spread out both her arms while dancing with a widening smile on her face. For a fraction of a second I seemed to see a tiny blue star shining on the top of her head. Some minutes later, having moved on to some other musical activity, she turned around and said: 'I love you!' I thought I'd melt on the spot. What an amazing change!

Before she left the CATTP, because she had reached the age limit of eight years, I said to her, 'Always remember that you can be happy when you dance. The little blue star I saw on your head the other day is actually yours and lives permanently in your heart.' Moments like this must not be forgotten and their crucial value should be recognised. Even if they last only a fraction of a second it may be enough to show us a way forward away from our suffering. In any therapeutic work, recognising the essential value of our qualities helps us not to miss those precious moments. If a patient can recall such a moment he or she holds the key to their further development in their own hands.

'Feather' was enthralled when one day a professional dancer came to the clinic to give a performance. Throughout the show she stood up and was commenting very excitedly on what the woman dancer was doing. It is not at all impossible that this little girl will one day become a professional dancer herself, a 'star', *une danseuse etoile*, as they say in French.

Observation shows that the *spiritual layer* is at the outer limit of our energy fields, approximately an arm's length from our physical body. The spiritual aura surrounds us completely and is made of the finest and fastest energy in our aura, which makes it the strongest and most penetrative energy available. It is in this layer that our *inborn qualities* are stored. They can be detected right from the moment of birth and are very likely acquired in previous lives. These qualities belong to the individual. No-one can take them away from us. They are ready to be used and expressed. It is up to us to activate them and to use them in our life. While our problems may temporarily conceal our qualities, they cannot damage them. We can learn to make active contact with them by directing our awareness to the individuality point or to the central part of the focus position, for instance. These energy structures are above our heads and their position is shown in Figure 1.1.

Our qualities are specific to each of us. There are seven types of quality, each one associated with a colour of the rainbow. Every person has at least one quality, more rarely someone has two. Deep within us we know all about our qualities, they are not foreign to us. They are our inner strengths with which we are familiar in a very natural way. For various reasons we may find it difficult to take them seriously and to express them. But when we do express them, use them, we somehow feel that we are on the right track. At such times our dreams may refer to them, their particular colour may appear in a detail in a dream. We may feel as though we are turning our sailing ship around into the wind and we can feel the wind filling its sails (Perret 1997).

Why is this spiritual layer located at the outer limit of our aura? How do we deepen our contact with it? What lies between this layer and our physical body? What happens in this space between the physical body and the spiritual or qualities layer?

Energy fields and their functions

The study of subtle anatomy and the energy fields is entirely absent from our education. Of course this does not mean that energy does not exist. As for anything else we want to understand, the study of energy takes time and dedication. Energy is a natural phenomenon. I have been studying it for over twenty-five years. It is a bit like studying the ocean or the climate, it is extremely complex and rich in information. Even after all these years I wish I knew more and understood it better. Very often at the beginning we do have to overcome a mental resistance to working with energy. Talking about energy verges on being a taboo subject and one meets prejudices and certainly a lot of ignorance.

It is just as absurd to consider energy to be something esoteric as it would be to treat quantum physics in the same way. Both lend themselves to scientific exploration and these two fields of interest are linked. There is an additional difficulty in talking about energy because some 80 per cent of what you may hear or read about the energy fields is lacking in common sense and humility. It is not unusual for someone claiming to work with energy to promise you the moon: all too frequently inaccurate information is offered. It has been picked up here and there and passed on without much discrimination, without ever having been verified. Taboo, lack of knowledge, energy's invisible character, ambition, greed and personal insecurity all contribute to the difficulties confronted in developing studies in energy which are sound and well grounded in experience. Therefore, I say, 'Don't believe what you read here, check it out for yourself, even if this should take you many years. Then you will arrive at your own understanding.'

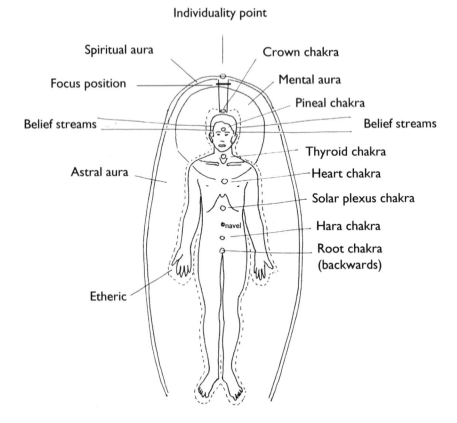

Figure 1.1 Energy fields and chakras

Of course, you do not have to study the energy fields. Many scientists do a marvellous job without seemingly using that dimension. Colwyn Trevarthen has told me that he does not feel the need to explore the energy fields, since he would find everything essential to his work, for example, by observing the subtleties in communication between mothers and their infants. His compassion and natural generosity, his sharp sense of observation allow him to take into account all the subtle dimensions without having to label them as 'energy'. I am convinced that all personal evolution goes hand in hand with compassion, with a capacity for detailed observation and with honesty. This will lead automatically towards the inclusion of subtle phenomena and that cannot occur without our intuition being at work. The fact is that the phenomena of subtle energy are part of our everyday life without us needing to label them as such. Many of our psychosomatic expressions refer to energy. So something may 'send shivers down my spine' or maybe 'I am feeling heavy' with a 'weight on my shoulders'. Perhaps I am 'feeling light-hearted' or someone I know gives me 'a pain in the neck'. We have 'a gut feeling' and sometimes there is 'a weight on my chest'.

If we deny the energy dimension in life serious consequences may follow. The increasingly obvious imbalance in and between the elements in nature in recent years could be one of them. Energy links everything together, human beings, plants, animals. It also connects the different levels and aspects within each of us, our thoughts, emotions, feelings, our physical body, as well as our deeper needs and spiritual dimension. An awareness of energy allows us to view the world, life and ourselves as being a part of an All-That-Is. Just as we cannot completely grasp phenomena on a molecular or atomic level without using a powerful microscope, we cannot understand and appreciate the subtle effects of sound without opening ourselves up to the notion of energy.

Each energy field is a complex phenomenon made of a number of structures, going beyond what we can explain in this book. Each energy fields has its specific function. Basically, energy relates us to All-There-Is. There is a continuous exchange going on between our energy system and all that happens around us, on all levels: etheric, emotional, mental and spiritual. Once we become aware of the existence of energy, we realise how much we are part of everything. Energy awareness teaches us what happens when we think we are separate and need not respect other beings, nature or other parts of the universe. Energy is in constant movement and transformation. Therefore we need to adapt ourselves constantly to these 'exterior' changes. When we resist change, harmony is interrupted. A blockage is created.

While describing some of the functions of our energy fields I am not trying to establish a theory. I am transmitting what I had the chance to study between 1979 and 1999 with Bob Moore (at the Psychic Centre in Ringkøbing, Denmark) through my own observations on myself and others, through reading about the Indian, Chinese, English and Tibetan Buddhist traditions. What I present here is only a reference grid that the reader needs to complete with their own observations. We need an understanding of the subtle anatomy of man in order to explore the role of the spiritual, the links between the different levels as well as the effects of sound on them. We are more than just a physical body and a brain.

We can have a physical illness or weakness in our physical body that needs healing. This can have been caused by a physical accident and/or an emotional shock, leaving its trace in our subconscious memory (which is part of our etheric energy field), in our emotional memory (the so-called astral aura or energy field) and very likely also on our way of thinking (mental aura). The cause may reach as far back as childhood, birth, pre-birth and even past lives. Healing these different levels probably needs a conscious effort to better understand how we function in relation to All-There-Is. The memory of each energy field helps to remind us of the cause of an unbalance and how we may have contributed to it. We need them in order to grow and sometimes change wrong decisions we have made in the past. It is a life-long study. All we are going to say about the energy fields, the brain, music or the five elements in this book therefore is a simplification. We had better bear this in mind.

In our *etheric* we store all the impressions we collect through our senses: visual, audial, touch, taste, etc. These different pieces of information are stored there without any discrimination, like in a photo album or in a storehouse. The etheric interpenetrates the physical body and extends some 12 to 15 cm outside of it. Our *subconscious memory* seems to be held in that storage, in- and outside the body. For example a memory of *a physical shock* registered on our foot will be stored in the etheric next to the bruise we got on the foot. Vice versa, blockages in the etheric can lead later on to physical trouble. Therefore detecting unusual energy accumulations in the etheric can help us prevent physical illness, if detected and worked with in time. Sometimes pain we feel can originate in other levels of our energy fields (as etheric, emotional or mental pain) and can be eased by working on that specific part of the aura. We can work with dispersing energy, re-establishing a flow with the help of sound or contact healing but very often we will have to combine it with directing more consciousness into that area. Pain automatically causes us to lay our hand on the spot, put some cream on it or blow on it – all of which is also directing consciousness to that area.

The emotional content of information related to a shock, for instance, is stored in the *emotional energy field* (or astral aura), which extends about arm-length from our body. This emotional layer – contrary to the etheric – works with an in-built mechanism of intelligence. The astral has a tendency to resist all changes. In other words we have, as we know, a hard time getting rid of emotional habits.

Thought structures that have been affected by an accident or shock, are stored in the mental aura. The links between these different memory places are most of the time unconscious. They can be activated though, sometimes through running into similar situations or through voluntary efforts, like awareness exercises, reflecting upon the event, talking about it and getting more clarity. The links then become conscious. The *mental energy field* (mental aura) stores our thoughts. The upper mental is roughly situated above our ears and eyebrows and stores clear thoughts, less infiltrated by emotions. The mental energy field reflects and conditions what is happening in the brain. Stress connected to intellectual thinking (often caused by emotional infiltration) can thus be detected and worked with – still simplifying – near the left hemisphere of the brain for instance. The mental energy field, when at rest, forms a bowl around the head as we can see represented on many orthodox icons or Buddhist paintings.

Realising that we have a presence beyond the simple limits of our physical body confronts us with many questions. Where does our personal energy field really end? Are we actually linked to the energy fields of other people, of plants, trees, the earth and why not of the stars and planets? What remains on an energy level after our physical death? From where do our inborn qualities come? Do they transfer from one life to another and if so how does this happen? Where is the seat of our spirit, of our 'I'? Where are our feelings generated? Energy fields are hugely complex and detailed and cannot be fully discussed in this book.

Consciousness growth

Socrates put it in two words: 'Know yourself'. This is the starting point for every therapist who will have to walk continuously along the path of self knowledge as long as he is working with people. This is absolutely necessary so as to observe, discern and understand oneself and others better. This cannot be done by reading books but only through working on oneself. Personally I use and suggest to others to use exercises for energy awareness and the development of the mind. These exercises help to develop intuition and enable discrimination between intuition and emotions. They help to improve our contact to our innate qualities and expand our understanding of what spirituality is (Perret 1997). We need to combine, for that purpose, the right and left sides of the brain, our feeling and analytical selves. We must observe what occurs with an open mind and with discernment. This search for consciousness growth has produced many schools and systems of teachings that have branched off from the more esoteric forms into some systematic and scientific approaches (Bertelsen 1982; Boadella 1987; Diolosa 2000; Perret 1997; Saraswati 2000; T.W. Rinpoche 2002).

This new scientific approach, combining intuition, feeling observation and intellectual analysis demands an open mind together with some serious sustained work on oneself. Consciousness growth invariably brings about deep changes for an individual. Bob Moore has written beautifully about this in the foreword to my previous book (Perret 1997). Our emotions know some sophisticated mechanisms of defence. Some 'hard nuts' are deeply rooted in our beliefs and can resist change for a long time. In all personal development we may at some point find ourselves up against a seemingly insurmountable wall. The obstruction to further growth will often be hidden in a fog of ideas telling us that it does not exist, that the problem is not really there, that we can ignore it, that it is too difficult to overcome, all this in order to make us turn back and not to face up to the challenge. Energy awareness exercises, like those Bob Moore taught can help us to move through such obstructions and to bring light into dead ends.

Musicality and consciousness

What is the role of music in all of this? What happens really when we improvise spontaneously? From where do the musical ideas come? What do we communicate in those moments? What is consciousness? What is conscience? Could one view musicality as a sensitivity that potentially allows us to express ourselves, and through doing this to bring to consciousness 'all' the dimensions of consciousness?

Musical expression has its source in different layers of consciousness: the lower astral where painful emotions reside; the upper astral where feelings of joy, compassion, peace, serenity and love are generated; the lower mental where intellect operates but often under the influence of the lower astral; the upper mental where intuition is at work; the individual's spiritual layer or soul and perhaps a collective spiritual layer. Consequently, any so-called *'creative' expression* is not necessarily what it purports to be. A lot of artistic expression is quite emotional and uninspiring. In order to understand what is actually involved in creative expressions of all kinds we need to go beyond simply noting what is happening to our brain's cells. What we see there are no more than physical manifestations of non-physical processes such as thought, imagination, feeling, emotion and intuition. We are much more than biological mechanisms. The neuroscientist Trevarthen opens a passage with these words:

> ...the act of playing music, and in a larger sense 'active musicality', are at the origin of the activation of states of consciousness and the development of intelligence, through the combination of an investigative curiosity and communication. (Trevarthen 2000a)

Listening to and playing music activates many different levels of consciousness (see Appendix 5 on the levels of experience). When following the laws of harmony, that is to say, respecting the various levels involved, music can facilitate communication and playful experimentation between the different levels of consciousness. To arrive at this point though, it is absolutely essential that our expression corresponds to our feelings. There must be a true and direct translation of any inspiration or feeling into musical expression. Thus musical expression becomes a part of the ongoing process of mind trying to catch up with and anticipate external and internal change. Musicians, whether amateurs or not, can themselves be viewed as an instrument. Their state of mind determines very much the level of consciousness transmitted through 'their' music. A player who has sufficiently worked on his or her painful emotions, and who is not governed by them any longer will naturally access other levels of consciousness.

Every human being is always on an evolutionary path, whether he is disabled or not, whether she is aware of it or not. During a summer camp with physically and learning disabled people in the Swiss valley of Simmental I was holding a music workshop for ten days. During group improvisations the people with special needs were sometimes more free and more creative than the staff. Our culture produces quite a number of analphabets in musical matters. The musical instruments I suggest for playing (see Appendix 1) allow anybody to create or to participate in creating 'sound paintings' with a great variety of 'colours' and 'shades'. Melody, rhythm, dissonance and harmony often lose their meaning, nothing sounds wrong.

Most sound paintings began in a very spontaneous way and might last up to an hour! One disabled person was asked to start in any way he wanted and even if the initial musical action seemed minimal, it would influence the rhythm, the intensity, the atmosphere, the loudness and the 'colours' which were chosen afterwards. Each sound painting was totally different from the other. In one we would swim through worlds of metallic sounds and small bells, cymbals, tubular bells, small gongs and other metallophones. In another we would find ourselves in a crystal cave and in yet another improvisation we would find ourselves celebrating an imaginary 'year of the dragon'. Then it might be dry, short sounds that would prevail, transporting us into a 'rainforest' full of strange noises.

Concentration, intensity and *joy* are sure signs of quality in the group work. It was neither virtuosity, nor loudness that created the feeling quality. Every person who played would discover with astonishment how much joy and musicality was pouring out of them and how easily their own music fitted in with everybody else's. The differences between the various disabled people disappeared. Everybody seemed washed away by a 'river of sound'. Someone's speech problem lost its importance since nobody was talking. Communication happened in the *space* between us. A fabric started to appear, woven with fine threads made of sounds and feelings.

This way of playing puts every participant on the same level. It is very rarely that anyone is left out. A communion happens and the participants' creativity is liberated. Where tolerance and self confidence can blossom, bridges are established between expression and the deeper layers of consciousness. These deeper feelings can bubble up and integrate consciousness in daily life. This may take some days, weeks or even months but eventually it will happen. During a free improvisation, everyone is somehow following her own thread of gentle craziness and no-one is pointing the finger at anyone else.

This gentle folly allows self-healing forces, the spiritual level in each one of us, to take over on a group level as well as on an individual level.

When intensity and joy are present, it is as if our soul was directly guiding our body and mind. These moments are of deep value as regards self acceptance and self realisation. They remind us of who we really are, of our deepest dreams and longings, of what nourishes our soul. They reveal us to ourselves as well as to others. These kinds of improvisation can help transform deeply rooted emotions and lead us towards serenity, a sense of freedom and can enable the individual to evolve as well as the group as a whole. In music therapy these spontaneous improvisations can be used with families in therapy, with a business team, a school class and in many other situations.

I have worked in institutions for learning disabled people where staff and parents had little awareness of the disabled person's need for personal development. Either the disabled people were cut off from expressing their feelings and needs by medical drugs or because of the absence of a therapeutic dimension. Only a minimum number of staff were employed just to ensure feeding and cleanliness. The tragic part of this situation was that these institutions were managed by the parents themselves. They had been motivated to provide material security for their disabled children but had forgotten their children's deeper needs for growth as well as their own needs for this.

Consciousness growth is not a luxury. While the spiritual aura is being nourished by experience and expression it is not the only aspect of us that benefits from this growth. Gradually all the layers of our energy fields become transformed. Growth means that the spiritual or light aspect or the higher level in us is taking over the steering wheel. Gradually the emotional layer loosens its grip and influence. The painful emotions are transformed when we make some room for feelings. The lower mental then becomes less clouded by emotional interference in our thinking. The upper mental and upper astral become more significant.

There are different definitions of mind. I tend to view *mind* as a conglomerate of the upper astral where our feelings reside, the upper mental levels, the individual spiritual level where our innate qualities are found together with the spiritual layers beyond the individual. Tibetan Buddhism describes the nature of mind by distinguishing between *sem*, the intellect known also as our lower mental field and *rigpa* or the ultimate essence of mind which is the basis for any abiding comprehension. These teachings suggest that only the experience of pure mind allows us to know the nature of absolute reality. 'It is simply your flawless, present awareness, cognizant and empty, naked and awake' (Rinpoche 1992, p.49). Buddhism is at the same time pragmatic and metaphysical in its approach to mind. 'No words can describe it…it has never been born…it has no limits at all' (Dudjom Rinpoche in Rinpoche 1992, p.49).

These definitions are clear, simple and at the same time open, thus taking into consideration the fact that we actually know very little when it comes to consciousness and the mind and that words are a very restrictive and inadequate means to express what we do know.

In Indian philosophy, essentially still present and alive in the millenary traditions of yoga and Hinduism, the definitions of consciousness and mind are very similar to the definitions in Buddhism. Buddhism incorporates huge chunks of Hinduism as well as rejecting certain central aspects of Hinduism such as the caste system. Buddhism was of course formed in the midst of Hindu culture. The reason why Buddhism, Hinduism and Chinese Taoism are such rich sources of understanding when it comes to the nature of mind, as well as for all that is beyond the physical and the visible, comes from the fact that the founders and practitioners of these traditions have been studying the subject for millennia and have no trouble accepting the existence of invisible energy. The encyclopedic dictionary of Yoga by Georg Feuerstein (1990) for instance offers us a rigorous and clear approach to the subject based fundamentally on pragmatic self observation. In the Indian tradition, the lower mental or intellect is called *manas*. In the yogic tradition *manas* is considered as a sense because of its close resemblance to the processes of the five senses. Accordingly, its operational ways are anchored in desire, willfulness, doubt, irresolution, shame and knowledge (I guess they mean 'received knowledge or opinion' here as opposed to personal knowledge), fear, belief, lack of belief and discipline. This makes of *manas* a suspect and unreliable tool.

The neuroscientist Antonio Damasio in his book *The Feeling of What Happens* (1999) ventured into a deep research of *consciousness* and its mechanisms. In it he reminds us of the necessity of making a distinction between 'mind', 'consciousness', 'moral conscience', 'soul' and the 'spiritual'. He believes that the consciousness of a person can be described as 'the real sense that a person has got of herself and her surroundings'. He suggests considering consciousness as being a part of mind, the conscious part. 'There can be mind without consciousness, as can be observed with patients that have got only one without the other.' After this observation he focuses on what consciousness is and how it is manifested on a brain level, warning us at the same time that 'Understanding consciousness says nothing or very little about the origin of the Universe, the meaning of life nor of their probable destinies.' Consciousness, according to Damasio, is at the beginning a feeling of what happens when we see, hear and touch. He underlines thus how much consciousness is anchored in our bodies and our physical sensations.

Bina John emphasises the point that to understand the link between music and mind, we need to include emotions in the definition of consciousness, the neurological as well as the spiritual aspects of the experience (John 2003). She is convinced that musical education must start from a feeling basis including experiences of a spiritual kind, those filled with meaning, so as to motivate young children to engage with music. Stanley Greenspan (1997) agrees that our emotional development is essential for any further form of development.

The definition of consciousness does not necessarily include any moral conscience (since moral conscience is only partially conscious), but does embrace a number of different levels of consciousness as well as the awareness of oneself. Consciousness is the *conscious part of mind* capable of observing phenomena that take place on different levels whether physical, emotional, mental or energetic and which relates them to the observing self. Consciousness has the faculty to be aware of itself, to associate with ourselves the observations we make about our body and our whole psycho-energetic system, and it can discern the differences in phenomena that do not concern us.

Again the explanations in Buddhist and Yogic traditions help to clarify the issue (Feuerstein 1990). They draw our attention to the numerous traps and illusions concerning our knowledge of the human mind. To find access to really liberated states of consciousness they suggest learning to stabilise five functions of mind and only then learning to detach oneself from them. These are exact perception of the material world, intellectual knowledge, conceptualisation or intellectually chewing over things, lethargy, laziness and sleepiness of mind and finally lexical memory. In this book the word 'spiritual' means the source of mind reaching beyond the human intellectual mind. In India the Hindu tradition calls it *atman*.

Music can influence all these levels without us necessarily getting ourselves stuck in emotions or intellectual thinking. The fact that music does not use spoken language contributes considerably to its potential to do this. Music can be a translation, more or less laborious, more or less trustworthy, of ideas, intuitions, inspirations and condensed impulses of a higher kind. For Damasio 'the basis or consciousness presents itself *in images and not in verbal form*' (1999). The translation into verbal language comes afterwards.

The specific qualities of this kind of musical expression contribute to the construction of a bridge between the mind and the spiritual. This will reveal to us the spirit's playful, poetic language and its power to activate our feelings. Experiencing the spiritual aspects within us will enable us to touch the deepest layers of our being. The *search for meaning*, to make sense of our life, individually or collectively, is the hidden motor behind our innate curiosity. A very evolved organism on an evolutionary level allows for the anticipation of changes. Music can help us find the deeper meaning in our lives. 'Musicality appears to be a human psychological process intimately linked with the unique intensity of the human being need to make, learn and transmit meaning in the experience of acting in common social experience' (Trevarthen 2000a).

When it is guided by the spiritual dimension, artistic expression allows the elaboration of individual and collective visions of who we really are and towards what we need to move in order to survive. As Caroly Bereznak Kenny (1996) writes in the *Nordic Journal of Music Therapy*: 'By elaborating our lives in music, we express our human conditions in qualities and musical patterns.' She underlines the enriching effects of artistic action in a large sense, allowing others to watch and participate, allowing empathy to surface between the players and the others which resonates in each person present.

Kimmo Lehtonen thinks that music is a kind of 'meta-thinking' (1994) that helps us to reach in a practical way all 'forms or structures of meaning' so as to integrate them through the creative musical act. He believes that active music making accelerates the psychic work and the individual's symbolic processes. The process in music therapy activates both the therapist's and the patient's subconscious and brings into the open material from the subconscious, for instance musical sounds, images and fantasies that would otherwise not become conscious. Later in this article he writes:

> ...The symbolic material presented during an intensive music therapy session is narrowly linked to the work with dreams and its images, because they have similar unconscious structures, condensed thoughts, mirror images, crab movements and images instead of thoughts, for example.

In my experience as an improviser in musical expression, I have experienced states of consciousness much vaster than I can understand. It is important to remember that the unconscious is made up of not only a *sub*conscious with its unresolved emotions but also of the *supra*conscious with its inexplicable spiritual contents or, to use a more neutral expression, the subconscious is a part of the energy around us.

When during playing I manage to open what I like to call a 'door of the mind' (Perret 1997), I can never really tell to where exactly this opening will lead me. When, for instance, I enter into the logic of a Balinese slendro scale on the concert harp, I find myself transported into a totally different way of playing. When playing an aulos scale, known also as the Schlesinger scale after the English archaeologist who discovered the scale on terra cotta flutes in Greece, on a koto, I have found myself in a *space* I have called the 'ancient Hebraic'. Other people present when I was playing also experienced the feeling of being transported into an unknown space.

The concept of energy fields allows us to accept – if not understand – the different sources of musical inspiration. For years on end we can easily go on drawing our inspiration from gross emotional levels coming either from other people or from ourselves. By becoming aware of the different levels of our inspirations and their respective qualities, we may then choose to express inspirations originating in the upper astral level where our feelings lie, from the upper mental level (where abstract but not intellectual music can originate) or from our spiritual levels. I do not agree with Kimmo Lethonen when he writes in another article in the *Nordic Journal of Music Therapy* that creative impulses are limited to attempts to resolve 'archaic problems' caused by deprivation in our early childhood.

That viewpoint is the prototype for most psychological thinking and it cannot conceive of spaces beyond traumata and emotional problems.

During one course a participant felt the need to clarify something in herself. A dream the previous night had suggested that she do it. She improvised on flowerpots. Very quickly she entered into an intensive stream of playing and I had the sudden feeling of being in the middle of hundreds of wild geese all lifting off together from the surface of a lake in order to continue their migration. The feeling was very vivid and I could hear the tremendous noise made by all those wings and cries all around me. Before this the woman had been describing an energy movement from her belly area to her heart and then to her head. The scene with the geese was emphasising and giving form to this very feeling. In Chapter 2 I relate how the water element is linked to our belly. The birds were rising up into the air element, symbolising the chest and heart area and were flying towards a destination they would reach in a few days. I concluded that in a few days or so the woman would become clearer about what she had been feeling during the course. Images containing symbols like this do not appear by chance. It is always worthwhile trying to make sense of them.

Music helps us respond with the right side of the brain and through this to gain access to other levels of consciousness. These more distant spaces are often difficult to grasp and describe with the more commonly used left brain reasoning. The fact that our brain has organised itself into two distinct hemispheres may underline the fact that this enables two distinct and separated ways of perception that would probably not arise if the brain was a unitary structure. The brain's right hemisphere embodies the heart's intelligence with its possibilities of perceiving energy, the invisible, feeling dimensions, the spiritual. The brain's left hemisphere facilitates the intellectual processes, rational intelligence, our ability to deal with everyday matters.

The effects of musical and other sounds on our energy fields

Sounds act upon our energy fields through the phenomenon of resonance because music, sounds, thoughts and emotions are all vibrating phenomena. The effects of sound are often subtle and complex (Perret

2005). Some interesting research has been done since the middle of the 1980s in a discipline called *bioacoustics*. Researchers are exploring the correspondences on a frequency level of physical organs, bones and muscles for example, with the impact of an identical sinusoidal sound source. Observations suggest that such a sound source can affect and heal an organ or muscle by being played at the injured part's natural frequency.

I believe that the effects of sound are for most of the time multiple and I would not be in favour of over simplifying the connection between a single sound played at a particular wavelength and the corresponding organ. It is quite evident that we are at the very beginning of a new or maybe of a very old science exploring the treatment of trauma through sound and colour. So we should remain humble and patient. Nevertheless there are a good number of publications by researchers, medical doctors, music therapists and sound healers who are slowly and sincerely investigating this field.

Some conventionally trained music therapists are quite defensive in discussions about the effects of sounds on people. This is probably because they have not been taught anything about this. Their lack of information means that they do not have satisfactory tools to detect the effects for themselves. They withdraw into scepticism. I am not myself in favour of mono-causal explanations when it comes to sound and its effects on us, rather I would encourage someone to learn to acquire new tools for making observations. The psycho-energetic approach has given good results and is a method of observation accessible to anyone. My own observations indicate that there are several factors to be taken into account. These are listed below.

Let us recall a basic truth. The immediate effect of sound on someone will largely depend on her background and her emotional reaction. Even if we could totally isolate the effect of a sound, I think that it is more than likely that we would observe several simultaneous effects. With experience, though, it is possible to anticipate certain types of effect. A deep drum for instance will almost always have an effect on the belly area and, depending on the other factors involved, would also produce effects in other places in the energy fields. This means that we might be able to observe and feel certain effects, but it is very likely that we would feel other effects only after some hours. The effects of sound can be felt up to thirty-six hours after a treatment. Impacts in an energy field take time to filter through into the etheric level and then into the physical level.

Even though there remains a lot of research to be done, I believe that it is possible to contribute to a person's overall harmonisation, or well-being, through the use of appropriate sounds, music and thoughts. My more than twenty years of experience, discussions with numerous researchers and the growing number of scientific publications appearing since 1990 make me believe this. The effects of sound go far beyond bringing about a simple state of relaxation. Like any psychotherapy, music therapy does not try to be a substitute for medicine, be it allopathic or homeopathic, occidental or traditional. As in all therapies the psychosomatic influence must be taken into consideration and for some people bringing about a better mental harmonisation is the key to the healing of the whole being.

Five factors determining the effects of sound

In any therapeutic work using sound one should be aware of these five factors at work:

1. The receptivity of the patient. Is she open for the treatment? Without it we would not get the necessary combination of consciousness and sound needed for any lasting beneficial change.

2. The attraction level of the healer/therapist. What is her motivation and level of contact with herself? This will determine the depth of the treatment.

3. The musical components involved. Rhythm, timbre, tonality and frequencies are among these.

4. The quality of the musical instrument or source of sound (Perret 2005).

5. The energies present in the room, place, persons and time of day and year.

The social, cultural and professional history of the persons involved are contained in the first two points.

Having had this close look at which level of consciousness may be discernable, we can proceed to see how to detect them in someone's musical expression. I would like to introduce for that purpose the five elements system which employs the elements earth, water, fire, air and space in a metaphorical way so as to further our understanding of our psycho-energetic make up.

Tonglen Painting

Prayer flags whipping against the wind
stretched against the cloudless sky
Om ma ni padme hum
Om ma ni padme hum
in waves out into the bright atmosphere
colours vibrating in the blue vastness.
A dancing singing expansion
into the ocean of suffering and pain.
The vajra mind, the diamond strength
sees this with an open heart
a still point that does not fear.
It is the wind that blows the prayer flags
that creates an immense space
that holds both suffering and joy
opening into shimmering oneness,
soaring into blue with the buzzard.

Marie Perret, 1999

Chapter 2

The Five Elements in Music

Qualitative observation

Numerous phenomena – especially musical ones – remain incomprehensible to the intellect, if one responds to them only with the left side of the brain. It is these phenomena that have always attracted me. I have therefore endeavoured to find ways to observe, discern and understand them better. I have listened to a great deal of non-melodic music that one may call *soundscapes* or sound paintings. They may particularly suit a qualitative approach. The more I listen, the more I can perceive ways of discerning differences in quality. To what is such discernment actually responding, since there is often no melody, no tonality and no rhythm in these soundscapes? In my training programme I let people listen, for instance, to recordings of six different didgeridoo players and six different musicians playing on singing bowls. Why do we perceive differences of quality with singing bowls? A bowl is struck from time to time, yet within seconds we get a clear impression emanating from the way they are played. This is not due to the quality of the bowls themselves, but rather to the way they are played.

On recordings of didgeridoos you can more or less hear just one note. The playing technique is roughly the same and not necessarily very varied. Yet again we may experience a clear sense of a distinct quality pouring out of every recording. The different qualities experienced cannot be explained logically. The first time I became puzzled by this phenomenon was when looking for a suitable version of the 'Gavotte en Rondo' taken from the partitas for solo violin by J.S. Bach. I went to a public library that luckily had five or six different versions of that Gavotte. While comparing them I realised how different the versions of this same musical score were. I finally chose a version played by Itzhak

Perlman, which I perceived to be the only one showing a very good balance between the male and female sides. Generally speaking our left side of the body is our receptive, feminine side, our link to emotions and feelings, to our inner reality. It relates to the right hemisphere of our brain. The right side refers to expression, the male aspect, the step we take towards something and is linked to the left hemisphere of the brain. How should I try to understand the difference of quality in all the versions to which I listened?

The same question arose when I listened to six different female singers interpreting songs by Saint Hildegard of Bingen. From the first seconds of each interpretation I was aware of distinct differences in quality. I could on many occasions verify with friends and course participants, musicians and non-musicians alike, that the perception of these differences was largely a common experience.

The first album of meditative music I ever composed was in 1981. I played on a superb Steinway grand piano and tried to catch the atmospheres of seven different trees. It is impossible to describe logically how to render the particular energy of a tree merely though music. I remember playing those recordings to a class of primary school children and asking them to draw what they heard and felt. They did not know which music represented which tree, yet they were able easily to detect which one was the birch and which one the oak. They were equally able to express their impressions using coloured pencils on paper.

In my courses I suggest that participants represent their impressions of one of their colleagues by improvising a soundscape type of music. I give them mostly non-melodic instruments to work with because they encourage the creation of sound paintings. I often give someone a specific task such as playing 'a mountain' or 'a large slow moving river', a task that can seem insurmountable at first. It is very interesting to discover how well most people are able to create in their playing the exact atmosphere of the subject given to them and that the listeners can actually pick up the very same image that I had whispered into the musician's ear before starting the exercise.

Using *metaphors, images* and *symbols* allows us to express dimensions that are largely unknown to the intellect. With their help we can grasp the mysterious, the magic at work. Although we sometimes believe we can catch the essence of a phenomenon with the help of words, we often realise later on that this is largely an illusion. However, there are certain words that can reveal a number of unexpected layers of understanding. This is well known in healing, cultural and religious traditions that have been using the system of the five elements for centuries if not millennia. Those who developed these systems knew that engaging with the five elements in a metaphorical way would somehow help them to express their glimpses of the mysterious. They also knew that anything they could say about any one of the elements, its correspondences on the physical and non-physical levels would be only 'finger pointing' in the right direction. The five element system would never serve to touch or represent the phenomenon itself. Accordingly, the use of symbols and metaphors may serve to bring us closer to the truth than we would get if we responded on a purely intellectual level.

In order to discern the quality of what is being played it is essential to listen and respond with the help of the right hemisphere of the brain, thus using feelings, intuition and overall impressions. After doing this we can bring into play the brain's left hemisphere to analyse what we have just heard with some precision. How do the processes of the right side of the brain work?

Thousand-year-old traditions

So as to understand and express laws operating in the natural world, mankind has evolved numerous models. One of these is the Chinese yin and yang system that lead to the development of a system named the five phases of energy, sometimes mistakenly called the five 'elements' system, a cornerstone of traditional Chinese medicine. I use the five elements system as known in Ancient Greece, in India and in Tibet. Since 1980, I have been developing this approach in my work as a music therapist with a great variety of people including people with special needs, prisoners, children and adults who come to my training programmes in different countries. I also use this approach in my work as a musician, as a music teacher and as a composer. As one of my principal sources of inspiration I would like to name Bob Moore. I have enjoyed books from the anthroposophic tradition as well as from Indian, Chinese and Tibetan traditions (Bertelsen 1982; Diolosa 2000; Gamborg 1998; Irwin 1988; K.T. Rinpoche 2002; Peukert 1976; Saraswati 2000; Satyasangananda 2000; T.W. Rinpoche 2002).

The ideal state of an element is its balance relative to the other four elements together with its own evolution towards a more spiritual level. Each element is then in a continuous dynamic of evolutionary change and is in an unending search for balance due to the constantly changing world in which it appears. We can easily observe the characteristics of a metaphorical element by noting how that element appears in nature. We refer to all the five elements together as a metaphor in order to understand better how they may function on an inner level. Each element exists within us in its emotional aspect. It can, though, be transformed into its feeling or spiritual counterpart.

The element *earth* for instance is strongly associated with any sense of 'insecurity' and its counterpart *security* and self acceptance. The *water* element is connected to anger which is opposed by *calmness* as well as by vitality and physical well-being. *Fire* is associated with fear and its counterpart the qualities of *love* and understanding. The *air* element may be used to discern either *joy* or depression and self pity and *space* element may reveal either suppression or its opposite the qualities of *expression* and silence (see Table 2.1).

In Tibetan medicine the same five elements are traditionally linked to the first five energy centres or chakras and to an ideal state of being that personal evolution aspires to attain (K.T. Rinpoche 2002). 'Chakra' is the name used in Hinduism for an energy centre (see Chapter 1). The five element metaphor gives an access to practices of inner transformation in the different Tibetan traditions, Buddhist, bön, dzogchen and tantra as well as in the Indian traditions, yoga, Buddhist and tantra. The roots of these traditions go back several millennia and they offer a very detailed understanding of the five elements and how they form our world.

In his book *The Tibetan Book of Living and Dying* Sogyal Rinpoche describes how in the Tibetan tradition the death process is viewed as a movement through five stages that correspond to the five elements. During this process the energy first leaves the earth element, our feet and legs until we cannot stand up any longer; then it leaves the water element and we lose control over the body's fluids; after this energy abandons the fire element, our body, becoming colder and colder. Energy remains for a while in the heart region and the lungs as the air element until, with the last laboured breaths, the energy leaves the body altogether (Rinpoche 1992).

The five elements system provides a fundamental metaphor that helps us to understand the dynamic that underlies different modern scientific disciplines such as chemistry, physics, medicine and psychology. Tenzin Wangyal Rinpoche writes:

> Through an understanding of the elements we can see that apparently different dimensions of experience are really only subtler and grosser levels of the elements. An excess of fire, for example, manifests in physical, energetic, mental and spiritual dimensions.

'So, fire is the life-giving energy of the sun as well as the life-destroying forest fire' (T.W. Rinpoche 2002, p.11). For Tenzin Wangyal fire is

> the heat of the digestive system, the creativity of the mind, the red light of the rainbow, the phenomenon of temperature, the emotions of hatred and desire, the warmth of compassion, the wisdom of discrimination, and one of the five most subtle and most fundamental aspects of being. (T.W. Rinpoche 2002, p.12)

The five element metaphor allows us to understand a number of phenomena. It allows us to glimpse the laws at work that gave us five fingers, five toes, five major senses, five major categories of emotions and their transformation into five positive aspects, among other things. In the Tibetan approach, again according to Tenzin Wangyal Rinpoche (2002), we can find a healing level that creates a bridge to the traditional Chinese medicine and its five major organs system: earth/spleen, water/kidneys, fire/liver, air/lungs, space/heart. These pairings link us to the psychosomatic dimension of each major organ which is so well described in Chinese medicine and one of its branches the science of acupuncture meridians.

Tenzin Wangyal Rinpoche also reminds us how each element may bring us pleasure and well-being. When we lose ourselves in the vastness of the blue sky or the starry night, it is the element of space that nourishes and regenerates us. The flight of the swallows or the hang-glider, the movement of the flags in the wind, the full sails of a large sailing ship, the clouds, they all fill us with the generosity of the wind and the element air. The flames of a camp fire and the light of a candle bring warmth and comfort. A walk on the edge of the water, the presence of a cascade, the rain on a summer's day, taking a shower or a bath, pacifies and purifies us. Seeing a mountain or a freshly ploughed field touches us deep within.

Table 2.1 The five elements and their correspondences

	Earth	Water	Fire	Air	Space
Quality of the element	Solid	Liquid	Heat, light, warmth	Light, invisible, free, flexible	Emptiness
Body zone	Feet→ sacrum	→Heat point, 3 fingers below navel	→Lower end of sternum	Chest	→Eyebrows
Type of energy	Masculine	Feminine	Masculine	Feminine	Unified
Tendency	Descending, adhesive	Descending, gathering	Ascending, expanding, ripening	Dispersing	Dissolving
Symbol	□	☽	△	○	⊙
Zodiac sign	♉ ♍ ♑	♓ ♋ ♏	♈ ♌ ♐	♒ ♊ ♎	
Musical characteristics	Basic structure	Lively rhythms	Radiating, dynamic	Fluctuation, melody, chords	Silence, space, not 'busy'
Chakra	Root	Hara	Solar plexus	Heart	Thyroid
Endocrine glands	Adrenals	Ovaries, testicles	Pancreas	Thymus	Thyroid
Location of chakra	Sacrum, at back	5 fingers below navel	Stomach	Middle of sternum	Throat
Reich's body blockage zones	Buttocks	Belly	Diaphragm	Chest	Neck
Sense	Smell	Taste	Sight	Touch	Hearing
Emotion	Insecurity	Anger	Fear	Depression	Suppression
Feeling	Security	Calm	Love, understanding	Joy	Expression
Quality	Stability, concentration	Vitality, creativity	Transformation of emotions	Inspiration	Essence, emptiness
Level	Physical	Etheric	Astral	Mental	Consciousness
Etheric layers	Life ether	Chemical ether	Light ether	Reflector/ warmth ether	

In my work as a music therapist I find myself continuously confronted with the perennial question: is my way of working effective? How can I grasp more accurately the quality of an individual's musical expression, the essence of his difficulties and, of course, the progress made in therapy? I feel this sense of urgency even more with young children, always aware that it will be much more difficult for them to catch up later on with 'normal' evolution as a result of the time lost because of behavioural patterns which were not remedied before the age of seven or eight.

The primary goals during the music therapy sessions are simple though. I believe it is essential to watch for any sign of *intensity* and *joy* in someone's musical expression. I have the impression that these two qualities work like keys that open doors and make anything possible. How are they connected to someone's development process? What obstructs someone from leading his or her life with intensity and joy? When I speak of joy, I speak of a direct contact with something in ourselves much deeper than our mundane concerns. Perhaps we make contact with what one calls the soul, a spiritual aspect in us. Detectable intensity seems to bear witness to the total involvement of an individual's essence with his action in the present moment. As soon as joy and intensity are present it would seem that the five resistances to personal evolution and to the discovery of new aspects in us, as taught in Buddhism, vanish: laziness, doubt, sleepiness, anger and restlessness.

Over the years I have come to appreciate the impressive usefulness of the five element system for the qualitative evaluation of musical expression. The elements metaphor allows us to discover the natural bridges that exist between music and the human being, between interior and exterior. It helps us to understand concretely how much musical expression is a 'fingerprint' of the musician, how much his music reflects his whole being. We can learn to detect connections between someone's musical expression and his thought structures, emotions, body areas (with energy blockages), between the subconscious and spirituality, between left and right brain appreciation which is to say between intellect and feeling or intuition. The five elements metaphor allows us to draw a map that connects the quality present in a person's expression, musical or non-musical with his psycho-energetic structure. This allows us better to understand the inner dimension, residing deep within every being. The works by the neurobiologist Colwyn Trevarthen on musicality, the brain and communication confirm this. I will return to this later.

The five elements tool works in two ways: we can use it as a starting point to help a person find a better balance between the elements within and in so doing the different levels, physical, emotional, mental and spiritual will be affected. My hypothesis suggests that a better harmonisation within a person brings about a better musicality, that is an improvement in the quality of her musical expression.

Not only can we see if someone has got fire or lacks earth or space in her musical expression, we can also tell if she is *warm-hearted*, has her feet on the *ground*, is *fluid* in her movements and her whole being.

> The way we speak, the colours we like, and the way we walk and move our hands are expressions of the elements and in all these we can, if we know what we are looking at, see which element or elements dominate us. (T.W. Rinpoche 2002, p.23)

Qualitative listening assisted by the five elements can also be helpful when working with couples, families or groups. Listening to people playing together will tell us whether they have a tendency to avoid one or more elements in their functioning. As this is about feeling an individual's or group's psycho-energetic aspect, observation with the help of the five elements does not have to be limited to playing a musical instrument. It works just as well with singing, movement, dance, talking and communication in general.

The four elements earth, water, fire and air have been known in Europe at least since the days of Ancient Greece. They are part of our culture. Many expressions in our everyday language refer to them. We meet the same first four elements in our horoscopes, where each one is associated with three signs of the zodiac. The number of planets you have in any element can give you an indication about the excess or lack of a particular element in your make-up. The traditional system using the four elements was taken up again by Paracelsus in the Middle Ages (a Swiss doctor, 1493–1541). He added to them the fifth element *space* or *ether*.

The need to feel connected to All-There-Is is a human characteristic. It is not, therefore, surprising that similar systems using elements metaphorically have been used in other cultures. The Chinese have for centuries used the five phases of energy transformation *wood, fire, earth, metal* and *water*, which places the human being in a *global context* between heaven and earth. The Chinese meridian system – energy channels throughout the body forming the bases for acupuncture and acupressure treatments – is narrowly linked to their system of the five phases of energy transformation and can tell us in great detail about the psychosomatic influences on our physical organs.

Anthroposophic medicine has investigated the connections between the planets and our physical organs, while the North American Indians developed a medicine wheel with reference to the four cardinal directions of North, South, East and West plus heaven and earth. Healing traditions in Tibet and India use our first four elements, adding like Paracelsus, the fifth element space. Placing ourselves in relationship with the basic aspects of existence, of the universe, of the myths of creation, connects us with a meaning in life and is a necessary framework for all healing work. We find this approach in sufism (Islamic mysticism), in the various forms of shamanism[1] in Asia, Africa and America as well as in the Celtic tradition. Music, song and dance have played a role in all this since the beginnings of time. As different as these systems may appear to be, all of them teach us how we can *re-establish a harmony* with the world around us and God knows how badly we need to do this! Therapy with the help of music and sounds works with the same approach and surely we are talking about the same harmony:

In music as in life?

When listening, observing and proceeding to a qualitative musical evaluation we cannot limit ourselves simply to collecting logical and measurable criteria. Of course these do have their function, but remain analytical and intellectual in nature, that is they are based in left side of the brain activity. We also have to talk about feeling, musicality, intuition, access to the unconscious or preconscious layers. These are aspects of right side of the brain activity which nowadays western science has great difficulty in

---

1   A range of traditional beliefs and practices, that involve the ability to diagnose and cure illness because of a special relationship with, or control over, spirits. This tradition has existed all over the world since prehistoric times.

integrating. Since music to a large extent activates the right hemisphere of the brain, music therapists cannot let themselves be disheartened by the cultural propensities to ignore right side of the brain attributes. Fortunately, an increasing number of researchers and scientists have ventured into these right-hand brain fields during the past two decades. Other cultures have done so for millennia. We are not alone.

The five elements form a progression from the most solid one – earth – to the most subtle – space. Conversely, coming from the element space, the elements get more and more solid. The Ancients tell us that this latter progression is exactly what brought about the creation of planet earth. The connections between the elements and the five lower energy centres relates each of them to a specific state of consciousness: earth to the physical level, water to the etheric layer, fire to the astral or emotional layer, air to mental consciousness and space to pure consciousness.

In music as in nature, the elements are always linked to each other. It is practically impossible to isolate one from another. For instance, earth may be *humid, cold, hot* or *dry* or it may have different combinations of these attributes such as *humid and cold* or *humid and hot.* Air can fan fire into life, when fire is strong enough; but if the fire is very small like a candle flame, air may extinguish it and the quality of fire will be changed. Let us not forget this interdependence while we look at the characteristics of each element.

Earth □

How can we hear and feel the element earth in someone's musical expression and how is it related to their psycho-energetic structure? The feet and legs, the pelvic area and lower back including the kidneys have a direct link to the element earth. A good contact with these parts of our body brings us the necessary grounding. People who are too speedy, too cerebral lack contact with the earth and are often missing some stable basis in their life or a sense of personal success. Such people may find it very hard to trust themselves, to develop self confidence and may often feel useless.

One of the reasons why such emotions arise is because those people have cut themselves off from their feelings and emotions. They create a blockage at the level of the diaphragm and the solar plexus. Their feelings and emotions get pushed down into the subconscious (water). The blockage interrupts the overall energy flow from head to feet and back again giving emotions too much power over thought processes and a person in this situation gets trapped in a vicious circle where the intellect is kept eternally busy through the interference of underlying emotions. Many of our so-called intellectual efforts are thus often being made under the influence of unacknowledged emotions.

Emotional shocks are experienced as a sort of earthquake inside us, that makes our knees and legs tremble. This weakens our contact with the earth. We can feel that someone is 'pulling the carpet from under our feet', a person may be considered as 'not having their feet on the ground' or having attitudes which 'are not down to earth' or they are people who 'cannot settle down'. Our spoken language acknowledges many links between our psycho-energetic functioning and the elements.

The basic qualities of the element earth are stability, permanence, heaviness and solidity – on a physical, mental and environmental level. Too much earth can result in wanting to sleep too much and in feeling heavy. Conversely if you have sleeping difficulties you may want to try the following exercise: while lying down in bed be very aware of your feet for some ten minutes and imagine yourself being covered by a warm layer of sand or fresh clean earth.

Each element influences the others and is influenced by them. We cannot isolate one from another. Earth generally contains some water. Water blends with earth and makes it fertile and malleable. If enough warmth (*fire*) is added and the earth is properly aired, everything will grow easily. On the contrary, if there is too much heat and not enough water, earth easily becomes a desert. *Earth* and *air* do not work well together. The wind can erode mountains, move dunes and blow away topsoil leaving barren land behind.

The earth element can take various symbolic forms. Each one will have its particular significance and will reveal a specific quality in our psycho-energetic make-up. It can take the form of a sandy beach, a dune, a stony desert, a rock, a mountain, a river bed, the foundations of a house, a cave suggesting a feminine, protective aspect, a freshly ploughed field, crystals or other precious stones indicating the influence of light or spiritual energy.

We often come into contact with animal symbols or with the energy of animals which live on or under the earth, snakes, mice and suchlike. They too will tell us part of the client's personal story. Shamans, psychoanalysts and dream workers have throughout the ages drawn information from such symbols.

Everything that is an aspect of the *foundation of our lives* is linked to the earth element. Among these aspects are our connections with our bodies, our home, our work, our security, our successes, money, our relationships at home and at work. Past lives come into it as well. The symbol used for this element is the square, the most solid structure for a building's foundations as can be seen in the base of a pyramid. This symbol contains the number four which is found in the number of 'petals' of the root chakra, the energy centre at the base of our spine. Our DNA code, carrier of our genetic information, is formed only by four 'letters' or basic elements. The Hartmann grid, named after the German geobiologist who discovered it, covers the entire earth with a grid of etheric energy lines, which are about 1.1 m apart. These energy lines form squares. The sense of smell is traditionally linked to the root chakra and brain scientists have revealed that the sense of smell, together with the sense of listening, are the first active senses in the unborn baby.

Our basic feelings about ourselves and the world around us often have their roots in early childhood, birth and pre-birth. Were we really wanted by our parents? Did they have the means to truly accept us as we were? Feeling accepted in those early stages of life is immensely helpful in our later expression. When non-acceptance is experienced the opposite situation is likely to arise and this may be at the origin of pathologies such as autism, psychotic states or other disharmonious evolutions. In the early history of an autistic child it is not rare to find the death of a parent or relative before or soon after his or her birth. If the adults close to the young child or unborn baby have been very emotional about the death and more particularly if the mother has been much absorbed by the event, the adults' attention may have been withdrawn from the unborn baby or infant for a number of weeks. This may have led the young being to feel abandoned for a period long enough to have affected the foundations of its life and through this his or her earth element. Marie Ainsworth, an English child psychiatrist underlines this in her scientific work. She has noted a number of personality profiles such as the 'secure' child with a stable base who is able to trust a motherly figure. However, in the absence of such a base an anxious, resistant or escaping child was the common result (Ainsworth *et al.* 1978).

In order to ground our thoughts and to be able to concentrate we need a good contact with the element earth. When our mental energy is not well anchored, it accumulates around the head area and slips out of our control. The reason for this is very often an interruption in the overall circulation of energy that should bring the energy down from the head to the feet and up again. Our feeling contact with strong emotions can be blocked at the solar plexus and the diaphragm in the fire area making it impossible for us to 'digest' the emotions. In other words we do not experience them in our belly region. When we improve our earth contact our mental energy can again take part in the overall flow of energy and this will include a conscious approach to our emotions. In musical expression a client will then be able, maybe for the first time in many years, to play continuously on one musical instrument for several minutes. Even if she were able to play for only twenty seconds, this may sometimes reveal a significant positive change.

We may want to consider how we take care of the earth itself. I feel the whole question of recycling or burying waste into the earth, surface mining, covering large surfaces with concrete and many other issues affect the earth element as a whole. This is not to be taken lightly and the consequences may soon be felt quite dramatically.

I like Matthew Fox's[2] way of linking the root chakra to our capacity to feel connected to the All-There-Is, to the Cosmos. Through our contact with the earth we do in fact come into contact with all creation. This chakra links us simultaneously to earth and heaven (Fox 2000).

When trying to activate someone's earth connection while playing music, we might choose a musical instrument that needs to be played standing up, such as a large drum. In so doing we are encouraging the person to breathe deeply down into their belly. This may start to soften a possible blockage in the diaphragm. Listening to a didgeridoo, large gongs and deep singing voices while directing our attention to the lower

---

2   Author and reviver of the tradition of creation spirituality.

part of our bodies can also help this softening process. I am convinced that a therapist can only help a client gain a better grounding if he himself is well grounded. Good grounding needs constant effort. Deficient grounding is rarely improved in one or two days.

There are awareness exercises to improve one's contact with the earth. These exercises direct our attention to our feet so as to link our feet with the root chakra and sometimes also the pineal chakra at the forehead. For example an exercise may combine slow deep breathing with movements such as shifting the body weight from one foot to the other in a repetitive rocking motion. In doing an exercise like this it is very important that our intention, of directing our thoughts to our left foot, for example, is followed by our feeling perception of what we observe when doing so.

The musical elements which help to improve one's contact with the earth and which give one a feeling of security are musical *structures* that consist of slow regular rhythms, a drone sound and minimalist style patterns. If you attach ribbons hung with small bells to a child's ankles, this will automatically draw the child's attention to his feet. Obviously massaging feet and legs, having hot foot baths and visualising one's feet buried in warm sand or earth, will improve one's earth contact.

Everyone has key thought structures which are the foundation of one's being and beliefs. If beliefs are not based on personal experience and personal convictions, they will not be properly grounded. If such thought structures and beliefs are questioned, challenged or modified, one may experience an emotional earthquake.

Let us remember here the mountain example mentioned earlier. The quality of a *mountain* is a symbol for the earth element. Opposite to the mountain quality is the quality of a *valley*. The mountain represents male qualities including stability, steadiness, solitude. At its summit the mountain has a connection to space and silence. The valley represents female qualities and is associated with movement, velocity, most rivers as well as roads and train lines are found in valleys, and with social life. When we wish to express a mountain musically, we need to contact the mountain qualities inside us and to strengthen them. If someone finds it difficult to imagine *earth* or a *mountain* and cannot feel connected to them, she must be allowed some time to become familiar with the image, to feel its qualities, to become aware of possible obstacles towards its expression within herself and to dissolve them. That is the therapeutic or human growth dimension in this work with the five elements. It is necessary to bring feelings and expression into a balance, into a kind of osmotic relationship where the feelings flow unfiltered into the expression. Engaging with the elements in their natural conditions teaches us all we need to know. It is far more interesting to do this than to read about it in print which is why I shall now stop writing about the *earth*.

WORKING SUGGESTIONS

Let the person you are working with play stable structures, a drone for instance, let him keep a steady rhythm, using his body while playing the instrument, beating a drum for instance. Check that the player is breathing deeply into the belly. You may tie ribbons hung with small bells around his ankles. Encourage the player to stamp his feet rhythmically and to play and dance bare footed.

Water ⌣

The water area extends from the pelvic area upwards to just underneath the navel. This is the area of the body with the highest percentage of water and with few bones, except for the spine. In this water area we find the hara, a main energy centre and the centre of gravity in the human body. Accordingly, this energy centre has great significance in Tai Chi and in all martial arts. The hara is strongly associated with our *instinctive intelligence*. Water cleanses and connects us to the elimination processes of our body.

The half moon symbol opening upwards forms a vessel able to receive water. The moon has a very particular link to water as the tidal movements reveal. Let us not forget the strong symbolic association between the moon and our subconscious which contrasts sharply with the symbolic association between the sun and our consciousness. The prone half moon draws our attention to its lowest point, a point of balance, for example between the male and female aspects in each of us, and a centre of gravity.

When we look at the four layers of the etheric we find a complementarity between water whose symbol is a semicircle and air whose symbol is a full circle. (See also explanations on the energy fields in Chapter 1.) The 'chemical ether', the innermost layer of the etheric field corresponding to the water element, will become incapable of nourishing our body's cells if the link with the outermost layer of the etheric, the 'reflector ether' corresponding to the air element, is not maintained. Matthew Fox also underlines the unifying aspect of water, the cup symbol and the hara chakra. This chakra unifies the opposed male and female principles and links with the 'feminist philosophy', according to his 'creation spirituality'. Water and air are considered to be feminine energies in ancient Indian wisdom, earth and fire as masculine energies.

The earth element, as already described, is symbolised by the mountain, the male triangle pointing upwards, whereas the element water can be symbolised by the valley, the female triangle pointing downwards. This triangle has the shape of a valley. Valleys receive spring waters, brooks and rivers and have themselves the quality of movement, of velocity, whereas mountains are stable and unmoving.

> The Spirit of the valley never dies.
> It is the mysterious female.
> The mysterious female knows
> The passage leading to Heaven and Earth
> Dimly visible,
> We guess its presence
> Yet use will never drain it.
>
> *(Lao Tse, Tao Te King, verse 6)*

The water area of the body is inseparable from the etheric energy field and its *subconscious memory*. This part of our psycho-energetic system is the key to our vitality, our sexuality and our creativity and it can be characterised in its emotional dimension with the energy of anger, which is nothing other than the suppression of our vital aspects. Someone who lives fully these natural aspects is usually calm, peaceful and is well connected to his body and sexuality. His movements and thoughts will be harmonious and *fluid*. He will be flexible and playful.

An ancient Indian philosophical tradition describes a progression of the five elements in the creation process of our world, starting with the element space or ether the least material element, finishing with the element earth the most dense and solid element. In the Indian tradition of thought each element is created by the previous element. Fire brings about an expansion that leads to a progressive cooling which will bring forth water. So water becomes the creative base of all physical manifestation, earth. If these thoughts seem strange us, we can remind ourselves how we were created in water, the amniotic fluid in our mother's womb. The myth of creation in the Hebrew bible follows the same steps. This may explain why the water area plays such a key role in our creative capacities.

Obstructions in the water area are not only apparent in body language but can also be recognised at a *symbolic* level. In a person's dreams, as well as in his imagination, water would then show itself in the form of ice, frost or snow and being hardened would not be able to move freely any more. These symbols of frozen, immobile water may be reflecting someone's rigid thought patterns and constrained body movements. Such a person might intuitively perceive stagnant water or a dam, maybe one about to burst, as well as images of sharks or crocodiles. Images of sea monsters may appear and these will be pointing out subconscious fears and aggressive thoughts. These fears may not only be revealed by the state of the water itself, but also by what is under the surface of the water. This is a familiar metaphor for our subconscious often used in fairy tales. Autistic people, for instance, have an ambiguous relationship to water and so to their own body. They may go through phases of intense fear about water, but may also be fascinated by the sound of running water in pipes for example, as if instinctively recognising their need to integrate this aspect.

We should carefully note images, impressions or dreams which present metallic structures associated with water. Such images symbolise the excessive interference by rigid thoughts in the water area. In this case the movements of the person will often be jerky rather than fluid, suggesting lack of tonicity and control. Such a person may beat a drum too violently without realising it, so I would usually take away any beater from the player and let her strike the drum with her bare hands. She would then become more aware of the violence within through the pain in her hands.

It is through the condition of the water element that we may better understand the mechanisms leading to *fascism*. Fascism is an opposing force to creativity. Fascist style education – still present to a greater or lesser degree in many families and schools and still widely considered to be a very efficient way of rearing children – is characterised by a lack of respect for the individual's needs marked by an insistence on obedience to external authority. This will more specifically have an influence on a person's water aspect. To encourage the unfolding of a person's creativity and individuality is very important. If we do this there will be fewer adolescent suicides, less depression and misuse of drugs that themselves bring about the suffocation of vitality and creativity.

To be of lasting benefit all transformation of the energy in an energy centre needs an influx of spiritual energy, energy that comes from beyond the emotional and mental levels. The inferior and destructive aspects of the hara chakra, the centre of the water area, such as anger, violence, sexuality, instinctive drives, fascist tendencies and subconscious influences, need to be placed under the control of the higher mental and spiritual aspects which are linked to an individual's quality aspects. It is obvious that beating on a drum only will not do the job. Hence the necessity, once someone desires a real transformation, for engaging in personal development through disciplined work with awareness exercises.

On a musical level the element water can be expressed through the capacity to move fluently and playfully from one musical idea to the next, through *lively and ever-changing rhythms*. The rhythm of water is different from a mere regular pulse. Pulse and unchanging rhythmical patterns belong to the earth element because they create stable *structures* and are *bases* for any musical development. When we see a river or a brook from an aeroplane, we notice that it characteristically meanders, revealing to us this natural movement of living rhythms. A river that is prevented from flowing naturally loses its capacity to cleanse its own bed.

Large, soft *hand drums*, whose skin is not stretched too tight, frame drums such as the Irish bodhran or the North African bendhir, talking drums, clay pot drums such as the Nigerian oudou or Indian gatham seem particularly appropriate instruments to help people access the element water. The physical effort required to play them is of course also helpful. To maintain a rhythm you must integrate it into your body's memory, the subconscious memory, and be able to play it from the hara, to play it from your guts. Traditional Chinese medicine has for centuries been suggesting drumming to help what they call the phase of energy transformation water and its natural link to the kidneys. The rainstick, the ocean drum and recordings of the sound of water, whether of waves at the sea shore, brooks, wells or rainfall, can be very useful in this context.

Trance-like rituals, based on dance and rhythms, have often been used as a means to restore balance in the water area. The different musical genres such as rap, techno, reggae and African music are a big comeback for rhythm. The fashionable djembes or other trance-inducing instruments such as the didgeridoo, document the search in our own culture and the difficulties it presents, to re-establish a natural contact with the element water. However, if the trance-inducing ritual includes too much hard metallic playing, often present in techno music, the conflict between hard jerkiness and fluidity will appear. I believe it is important to emphasise the conscious aspect in trance dance and respect for individuality in contrast to group or mass rituals and movements where individual expression is neglected.

Someone's water quality can be observed through the intermediary of involuntary associations, images, watery feelings and aquatic animals (dolphins, whales, fish, etc.). This perception engages the right hemisphere of the brain and is therefore not logical or analytical in nature so it may take a bit of practice. It is a *soft, peripheral observation*, as though watching from the corner of your eyes, which will lead you into this kind of feeling listening. The details of internal images can be quite eloquent. All have their particular significance. Not only do they provide information on the nature of a person's particular problem, but also on her own healing potential, ready to be activated. As in all therapeutic work, we need to distinguish between our own projections, that is, interference by our own emotions, and what is really happening within the patient.

Musical improvisations guided by imagery through instructions given in advance or during playing can be very helpful in the process. We can, for instance, suggest to someone to move out of some stagnant water towards clean running water. Suggesting the image of a dolphin, a whale or a seahorse can help someone to enter the depths beneath the water's surface. One can also be helped – why not – by imagining the sun's rays lighting up the underwater world. It is always very surprising to recognise with what precision such an image brings about the feeling of an element in the quality of the music played or sung. Sometimes when working with a group of people I would whisper an image to two or three participants for them to express in their improvisation. Often I let the other participants listen, respond to their feelings and draw. The concordance between their drawings and the original whispered image, unknown to them, is very often unexpected. A task like this cannot be carried out using our logical brain. What is required is the musicians' feeling capacity, their spontaneous, uncensored expression.

Working with *visualisations* or images popping up from the subconscious is very similar to working with dream interpretation. At first, when someone connects with her imaginative capacity and feels or sees images coming up from inside, she may be quite faint. This stage can evolve quite quickly and other aspects may come in. One thing that fascinates me is that beyond the person's primary focus on a foreground scene, she can access a wealth of information in her peripheral vision. You may ask her questions about the surrounding circumstances, such as the weather, the light conditions, the landscape behind her; whether there are any animals or persons present; what is happening behind her back, what is the feeling of the scene? The person will often be able to answer those questions with certainty. Knowing exactly where objects or persons are in the scenery or what shades of colour are present is also most significant. Is the little brook on her left- or right-hand side? Imagined scenes and images are not composed at random. They are very precise and, if it is necessary, lend themselves to detailed interpretation.

Some very astonishing encounters can happen. During one course I suggested that participants lie down and let themselves be carried away by the drum music I was playing. At one moment I had the impression of a very gentle wild animal approaching the scene and walking around us silently. Then it seemed to sit down next to a woman and remained there looking away from her. Normally I would let such an impression pass without attaching too much importance to it at the particular moment. What surprised me was the woman's account of her own experience. She had felt the paws of a light animal walking all over her belly, then over her chest area, as if a large cat had climbed over her.

Another time, during a course I gave in Copenhagen, I suggested to a woman of about sixty to launch into a free improvisation using one of the easy instruments placed in the middle of the group circle (see the list of instruments in Appendix 1). She chose an African mbira or thumb piano. Instead of plucking its fine blades she turned it upside down and started to slap on it with the palm of her hand. The instrument started to resonate with all its blades. Within a very few seconds an intense atmosphere was established. I then had the strong impression that this woman was at that very moment completely in tune with nature. It felt to me as though she was surrounded by the kind of tundra you can find in the far north. I felt the presence of a large animal. I could not tell whether or not it was an elk. I just knew he was big. When she had finished playing we shared our observations and impressions. Someone briefly talked about an elephant then stopped.

After that the woman who had played so beautifully told us something that had happened to her several months ago. She was woken up once in the middle of the night by what she felt was the trumpeting of an elephant. She was living somewhere in the Danish countryside and so she thought that it was somewhat embarrassing to hear a distant elephant somewhere in Denmark far away from any town. Next morning she got a phone call from her son who told her that he had just been sitting with his son on a beach somewhere else in Denmark, when a small elephant had approached them from behind. This had given the little boy a wonderful thrill.

This series of coincidences could easily be discarded as being haphazard and unworthy of attention. But in the context of this way of working, there was no sense in not considering them for a moment. Why had three persons in the group reported a similar impression, especially in the context of Denmark? I was convinced that there was important information in all of this especially for the woman concerned. I gave her my impression, telling her that I felt she had a great sensitivity which she had to take seriously, that she had a rare gift of tuning into nature and the animal world. Such a gift is seldom used in our days and it was very likely that she could use this gift for the benefit of other people. It was most likely that she needed to express this gift which would also take her a step further along her own path.

Let us come back to water. Harmonisation in our water dimension only happens when we bring our male and female sides into a better balance, that is balancing feelings and expression, instinctual and rational responses, emotional and mental states. Improving deep belly breathing will help to bring about this balance, as will massage and dance for both of these connect us to rhythm. People who avoid these aspects of their water element suppress essential and vital parts of their being and are very likely to get trapped in subconscious vicious emotional circles that can get quite out of control. People suffering from schizophrenia are conspicuous victims of these mechanisms. Their etheric aspect is considerably enlarged in the water area of their body. This suggests that they are hiding their emotions out of sight of their consciousness and away from their physical reality. Suppressed expression contains emotional energy and the subconscious memory as well as the thought structures connected with this. It is often held in the body around the thighs, hips and pelvic area – that is the water area.

Personal development seeks an overall harmonisation, that is to say a natural balance between all the different levels within us. None of the levels should be discarded, so working on our water aspect is a complex matter. It is associated with work on the hara chakra of course. The words 'chakra' and 'energy' are unfortunately often used by people who have no idea of the complexity involved in those phenomena. This often results in promises being given to balance or heal all the chakra centres in one weekend, which is a completely unrealistic promise. It is not as easy as that. Here I have underlined the multidimensional nature of the subject and anyone who has undertaken serious work on any chakra and the different problems presented in so doing knows this. The difficult things are to become aware of one's own blind spots and dead ends, to learn a set of exercises and to generate the will to practice them conscientiously so as to illuminate and clarify these difficulties.

Working on our water element can take our development a long way. We may start with wanting to overcome our fear of water, or wanting to become aware of our resistance to imagining any space below the surface, perhaps because of the crocodiles or other sea monsters we might meet down there. Even establishing a balance between our male and female aspects is quite an achievement. It often takes time. It is very often an initiation where 'the path is the goal', which is to say that the disciplined 'walking along' towards the desired result is all that counts. It is especially important when working on one's water aspect to slowly dissolve all hardness towards oneself, remembering that it is just this hardness of thought interference that disturbs the rhythm of water, the rhythm of life. This hardness is often symbolised in images of ice, snow, dams and all kinds of metal structures appearing in or near water.

Take a short moment to reflect on what we humans have done to our rivers. Intensive agriculture whose heavy tractors have compressed and compacted the earth, has at the same time created vast fields with no hedges or other brakes where rain water now runs down very fast with little time to soak into the ground. This, together with deforestation is one of the reasons for recent world-wide spectacular floods. Like all the other elements comprising our planet, the water element is out of balance.

On a symbolic level, *dreams* of huge tidal waves usually announce something 'big' from the subconscious surfacing into consciousness in the near future. We had better prepare ourselves for this, watching our dreams, doing some extra grounding exercises and working on a good body contact. To understand the natural way of water we need only pour a jug of water onto some outdoor tiles. Water will always find a way out which eventually will bring it back to union with the ocean. In the course of finding its way, water shows considerable creativity and ingenuity.

Musical expression helps the inner development work provided one proceeds with gentleness and takes the time required.

WORKING SUGGESTIONS

Does the patient or pupil express his or her vitality? Does she or he have access musically to their female aspect (left side, left hand, left foot) and to their male side (right side, hand and foot)? Can she move fluently from one musical idea to the next or does she get stuck with a single idea? Are her actions hard, abrupt or violent? Does she mistreat the instruments?

Slow uneven rhythms of say three, five or seven beats seem to me to be especially helpful in bringing about a better contact with the belly area. These rhythms lead to a natural swaying of the body from side to side to emphasise the beat which alternates from side to side continuously.

Guided imagery with the little brook

W. a woman in her thirties, had some difficulties in contacting her water area. She felt quickly overwhelmed by destructive, angry emotions. It seemed evident to me that she concealed an underlying pain that she needed to release. She had in fact had several abortions of whose pains of various kinds she had not completely let go. In the pauses during the workshop I often saw her playing on the balafon in a dreamy way, with little intensity. I asked her later on to go to the balafon and play a little river. Her playing was quite mechanical and needed more playfulness, while intensity was still missing. I suggested that she imagine more water coming down in that little river, to let the water flow around strongly, jumping over the stones in the riverbed. Seeing that she still could not invest herself fully in the activity, I suggested she tried again more playfully by imagining a leaf being carried down by the flowing water, or a child's little paper boat bouncing along. Her play became more intense. Then I suggested that she imagine rays of sunlight penetrating the surface of the water, illuminating the stones down in the riverbed. Her play became lighter but still not free flowing like a babbling brook.

My next idea was to ask her to let the river reach the shore of a little lake and to allow her attention to glide under the surface of the water so as to explore its depth. She said she felt more and more surrounded by darkness, yet at the same time she was feeling more secure. Her playing mirrored her experience. It felt deeper and more assured. The mechanical aspect present in her playing at the start had completely gone. She felt ready to meet some hidden aspects of her water element. The following night she dreamed that she was sitting on a toilet losing a lot of blood from her womb. This seemed to be a clear symbol of her willingness to acknowledge and to let go some of her painful personal history. During the previous days we had all worked with energy exercises designed to bring more light and clarity into the area below the navel. As so often happens, it was the combination of concentration of thought and feeling awareness that brought about the depth of work one can reach through musical expression.

Fire △

The symbol for the fire element is a triangle pointing upwards, a male triangle. It reminds us of the prism that allows light to be separated into its component colours. It reminds us also of the bottom level with its two opposite aspects and the third one, the controlling aspect being on a higher level, the top of the triangle.

For most of us, using the analytical left hemisphere of our brain presents no difficulty. However, because we use it so commonly we often have great difficulty in recognising and responding to the other, more intuitive right hemisphere of our brain. This is surprising because music does stimulate the brain's right hemisphere very well. Music arouses all our feeling aspects. One part of the explanation for the unbalanced use of our brain's two hemispheres is associated with our contact to our personal fire element as well as to our culture's general attitude to the fire element.

Should we not include in our understanding of the fire element the way our societies characteristically handle fire. We permit nuclear power installations, the manufacture of military firearms and weapons of all kinds and the burning of fossil fuels. There have been more suicidal actions with explosives, terrorist attacks using explosives and more forest fires in recent years. Parallel to all this have we not banned fire from our homes and towns: fewer and fewer fireplaces, the Christmas tree's candles changed into electric light bulbs. Did this happen by chance? We are afraid of fire. Fear is precisely the emotion that is linked to the fire area. There is of course a strong link between the mechanisms of fear and anger. The first reaction to getting flooded by other people's emotions is fear (or its opposites: love and understanding). Feeling fear then often generates anger if the person has access to the hara, since the power of anger comes from the belly area, the hara.

The fire area of the body lies between the navel and the lower end of the sternum. When we speak of fire, we are talking about transformation, be it on a digestive level in heartburn, in dreams or in emotional experiences. We may also experience a burning sensation in the solar plexus area when we wake up from a nightmare which presented us with intensely fearful and bewildering situations.

The energy centre at the *solar plexus* is where other people's emotions enter into us. Someone who has not learned how to protect himself well enough may be smothered by these incoming emotions which are often very powerful. Consequently, sooner or later, most of us will try to cut off our experience of these emotions by blocking our breathing at the solar plexus level. This prevents the painful experiences of these emotions from descending into the belly and guts, which act as a sort of resonance box for emotions. If we feel fearful of and threatened by other people's reactions, a common experience in childhood, when we want to express our own feelings, we start to numb our awareness of our emotional experiences. In spite of doing this, the emotions will continue to be active but will remain in the subconscious, beyond conscious control. This can be the foundation of a constant, uncontrollable feeling of fear of being overwhelmed by yet more emotions.

People who are dominated by fear lack warmth in their expression, they stay cool. Unfortunately these defence mechanisms can establish themselves rather early in life and they may bring about a slowing down or an underdevelopment of certain centres in the brain, especially in the frontal lobe. This often allows serious behavioural troubles to take hold, autism, psychosis and other pervasive development disorders for example. The navel with its obvious link to the prenatal and postnatal period is part of the fire area. We can readily distinguish four collective fears: fear of sexuality, fear of mental illness, fear of physical illness and fear of death. This gives us quite a range of themes with which to work when dealing with the fire element. The basic transformation of emotions happens when we can accept who we are with our entire personal history, our weaknesses *and* our strengths.

Fire is essential to *transform* emotions into feelings. The opposite experiences to fear are *love, understanding* and *acceptance*. There is a strong link between the astral field and the solar plexus centre. The transforming fire element also brings about ripening and maturation which are transformation processes.

When an energy blockage in the lower area of the body is dissolved a wave of heat may be generated. Like all other heat forms it will rise up through the body. Transforming emotions releases energy which can be used in the heart centre, that is in the air area of the body. This is discussed below. Fire also brings us into contact with *light*. This is a very important component in the transformation process, since light is linked to the influx of spiritual energy. Thus fire brings about moments of light and hope. It is light that enables us to see objects around us and which symbolically reveals to us a direction for our life (Satyasangananda 2000).

In the evolutionary conception of the elements it is air that is the origin of fire. Consciousness perceives objects for the first time and becomes aware of itself, realising that it is a separate entity. In Indian philosophical tradition this phase corresponds to the onset of ego, the sense of a separate, enduring self. It is not surprising, therefore, that there are strong links between the solar plexus centre, the sense of sight, the ego, emotions, the lower mental field and its emotional and intellectual content. The lower mental field can be widely infiltrated by emotions and can be used to block emotional experiences. Our sense of sight can be disturbed at times by what is happening in the solar plexus. Sometimes our sight becomes blurred when we look into someone else's eyes. This can be a clear sign that there are emotions present affecting the solar plexus area and that some confusion is about.

We can quite easily detect in someone's musical expression a poor contact with his fire element. The musical expression is stale, superficial, foggy, boring, perhaps lacking structure or being too rigid. Do not forget that a deficiency in one element may very well cause an imbalance in the other elements. Well-being is all a matter of balance and inter-connectedness. When someone's expression lacks warmth and radiation, listening to her playing does not warm our hearts.

> If we are dominated by fire, for example, then we try to activate water or earth, and vice versa. If earth is dominant – we are dull, sleepy, heavy – then we activate air or fire. And if air dominates us – we are flighty, nervous, with a short attention span – then we activate earth or water. (T.W. Rinpoche 2002, p.22)

Daily life is full of examples of this constant search for balance, we drink water when we are dry, hot and thirsty, we cool ourselves with cold, wet flannels when we are feverish. The weather, certain emotions and thoughts, what we eat, an illness, a draught of air, people we meet, noise, pollution, almost anything can cause an imbalance in the elements or conversely can help us to restore them to balance.

While the element earth can be seen in musical structures, water will be recognised by lively, slightly ever changing rhythms, fire will be heard in the dynamic aspects of music changing volume from soft to loud. We will feel fire through the *warmth* and the *radiation* in expression. Thera-peutic work on a large drum, using one's voice, or playing on a cymbal, small metallic percussion or a gong can be very beneficial, providing one is not forcing it and is staying connected to one's feelings. It is interesting to see how many people who have unresolved problems in the solar plexus feel irritable and even attacked by these metallic sounds.

On an imaginary level we can suggest to someone to imitate a lion's roar, to play the fire-spitting dragon or to imitate lightning and thunder.

As soon as the person has integrated that dimension, then we can suggest to her to express warmth, radiation, a sunrise, the gentle warmth of a candle, a fire's embers, the warm sand on which we may lie down. Using our imagination is a very important aspect for any intuitive observation. It is one part of our feelings, of the perception of our brain's right hemisphere.

When we become accustomed to noting how our everyday language refers to the elements, to noting other people's quality of expression and when we let ourselves develop a feeling awareness of these phenomena, the suggested parallels will become clearer and more obvious. The mechanisms of the solar plexus are complex and especially so because some of our fears are actually deeply rooted. Consequently, our automatic reactions will often be ruled by prejudices. Our mental defence mechanisms are subtle as revealed in some of our thinking habits and we should not underestimate them, neither in ourselves nor in others. How often do we let habits and fears govern our communications rather than letting love and generosity express themselves? Our emotional structures have their own intelligence and are inclined to resist when we want to change them. The transformation work with the fire element needs continuous effort.

Interpreting the symbols for fire that appear in our *dreams* can be very useful. Fire can destroy and in so doing may transform matter towards a non-material form. It is a catalyst that brings about change, renewal and evolution. Like earth, fire is a male or positive energy electrically speaking. Water and air are female, absorbant or negative energies. The images in our subconscious tell us whether we are in a process of purification and real change or whether our inner fire is being smothered. In order to control fire in a productive sense we need the help of the element earth as a container and to provide strength and fuel together with water to cool it, to extinguish it or at least slow it down if necessary. Fire also needs air to stimulate it.

Observing the parallels with real fire is revealing. To contain an open air fire we would build a stone circle around it and at home we use a hearth or a fireplace (earth). Even electricity (fire) is run through wires (earth). Studying the elements in their natural conditions helps us to understand how to balance them within us.

WORKING SUGGESTIONS

Is the person afraid of certain types of sound? Could this indicate an excessive vulnerability in the solar plexus area and the nervous system? Is she showing warmth in her expression? Does she have the tendency to want to control everything because she fears feeling empty and powerless because of her lack of creativity and inability to feel her emotions? We can try using the 'lion's roar', 'the dragon's rage', 'thunder and lightning', or 'the candle's light', 'fanning the embers into life', 'a baking oven', 'the heating', 'a sunrise or sunset', 'a warm beach'.

Instruments which can help the player to access his fire element are xylophones and the African balafon (both when played with hard mallets), wood blocks, castanets, foot rattles, bell ribbons, maracas, guiro, chascas, cymbals, singing bowls, bells, gongs, drums, clapsticks. Using the voice is also quite an effective instrument for working on the fire aspect.

Working with fire can help someone find the gateway into emotions stored away in the bottom areas of the body, water and earth. I have worked with a boy in music therapy who always felt tired after only ten minutes or so. He got in touch with his vitality and creativity for the first time in music therapy only when I insisted on working for a while with fire on a big drum while he used his voice at the same time. That day he started to use his whole body while playing.

Air ○

The symbol for the air element is a circle which has throughout the ages been used as a symbol for unity, for the All-There-Is, the universe, the spiritual dimension. The air zone in our body corresponds to our chest area including the lungs and the heart. The air element and the lungs are involved in exchanges between the inner and the outer, the near and the far, above and below, spirit and matter, myself and others. The element air links everything, puts everything into relationship and is concerned with different kinds of communication. It allows the spirit to see things from a different angle by stepping back a bit, by looking from a bird's eye view. It is scarcely surprising, therefore, that the air element and the heart chakra are our doors to the spiritual dimension, to greater freedom, to compassion and to our eternal source.

This air area is very sensitive to the *spiritual dimension* in our lives. When we neglect it depression is not far off. We feel a weight on our chest. The human immune system is under the influence of the thymus gland found just behind the sternum. Its effectiveness depends very much on a good balance in the air element. The root of the word 'thymus' is in the ancient Greek word 'thumos' which means 'seat of passion'. So the air zone is related to what we feel passionate about, what makes us tick. In the Tibetan Buddhist tradition air provides us with the necessary speed to change an emotion rapidly into its positive feeling aspect.

Can we hear and sense the air element in musical expression? Can we detect a player who is depressed or weighed down? The air element knows two extremes, the manic state or 'high pressure' in meteorological language and depression or 'low pressure'. The soaring movements in a melody, the lightness in a person's playing can make us feel the presence of the element air. Musical instruments that can help someone to find access to his air element are flutes and the monocorde which I write about further on. Singing and using our arms and hands in accompaniment to music can also be very useful. In general all music instruments that are designed to express *melodies* will facilitate contact with the air element such as the violin, piano, keyboard and accordion. Brass instruments predictably influence the fire area. Metal percussion instruments do have a strong connection to the air area and the mental aura that starts at the heart (see Chapter 1). Traditional Chinese medicine recommends working with gongs, bells, singing bowls and tubular bells for the metal/lungs area which corresponds in this respect with our air element. Metallic sounds trigger a natural expansion of consciousness.

The flute is a wind instrument and those who play it always risk to some extent, if they are not careful, losing their earth contact, or grounding, when playing it. There is a tendency to 'fly off', to cut oneself off from one's feet and legs. You can sometimes detect this in a flautist's playing. While listening to flute playing we might start to feel woozy. The musician's playing can become too airy. She may get lost in the space. We play who we are.

An imbalance in this part of our psycho-energetic system can come from thought structures rooted in early childhood. This early period of life can especially affect the upper chest area between the level of the nipples and the collar bones, which area includes the thymus gland. The death of a close person, if inadequately mourned will also have an affect on the same area. Feeling sorry for oneself or getting into a depressive withdrawal may well be tactics employed by the air element. Expressions of joy and compassion would be the antidote to these tactics. It is essential to free oneself from anything that weighs heavily on one's heart such as the stress, resentment and bitterness that one may hold on to after having been deceived.

Many emotions such as hatred or feeling rejected, even though first affecting other areas of the body, will eventually end up affecting the heart chakra and the physical heart. In such a condition we will feel weighed down and depressed and will certainly find it difficult to be carried away by our dreams and inspiration. The words 'inspiration' and 'aspiration' remind us that the Latin root *spirare* relates to breathing, both in the physical and symbolic sense.

In order to *transform the emotions* held on to in this area of the body and in the psycho-energetic system we must call upon *spi*ritual energy. There are two subtle channels for incoming inspiration that meet at the heart chakra. They originate beyond our energy fields, approaching us over the collar bones. I noticed these lines in a Tibetan thangka (a religious painting on fabric) picturing the medicine Buddha. They form a female triangle where the lowest point is at the heart chakra. This inspirational movement is the necessary counterpart to the transformation of emotions, a process that finishes at the heart chakra. Inspirations are actually felt in the heart area. The thymus gland that is thought by the western conventional medical profession to atrophy at puberty, does so only if it does not get adequate spiritual energy.

'Air' is in continuous movement. Movement, *fluctuations*, accelerations, slowing down and melodies are the musical clues to this element. We talk about melodies that 'carry us away', that 'uplift us', that 'raise our spirits', that 'give us wings'. Melodies invite us, like no other musical component, to raise our arms and hands in readiness for the dance. Hands and the sense of touch are closely connected to the heart chakra. We quickly realise it if a certain musical interpretation gives us a sense of freedom and lightness, or conversely if it evokes heavy sensations in us and we do not experience uplifting feelings. We soon know whether a player is giving us a sense of deep joy and inspiration or if she is just rousing our superficial reactions. Even when the title to a piece may associate itself with the air element, this may be nothing more than a good intention.

Birds, most particularly eagles, and big sailing boats are two other important symbols for the air element. They remind us of our deep connections to the sky, to heaven and to the distant shores of the land of our dreams. We feel that the bird is symbolically closer to the Divine. The bird represents the messenger between the lower and higher dimensions of existence. We may sometimes envy them because they have a wide overview of the scenes below them. Who has not felt the need to rise above daily worries so as to get back to the essentials of existence? The symbol of the flying bird relates to the two elements air and space.

WORKING SUGGESTIONS

Does the person feel light-hearted, does she take wing when she plays and moves? Is there melodic and harmonic sensitivity in her playing, a sense of beauty, of joy? Does she have a pattern of depressive withdrawals?

Ask the person to play the 'eagle', 'the wind', 'fast spiralling movements of air and leaves in autumn' or 'a feather that gently glides down to earth'.

Space ⊙

How can we be more aware of 'space' than when it is absent? People who are continuously busy and in an agitated state and who always seem to want to produce noise on an instrument, who cannot grant themselves or others any moment of silence, these are the people who lack space. They have not found their true centre. Space is an obvious quality which surrounds us on a mountain top or when we are gazing up into the vast blue sky. We can experience it when walking across a large plain, when watching the surface of a big lake or staring at the horizon. In such situations we can let ourselves sink into space, be absorbed by it while feeling it within us too. The element space reminds us of consciousness, of the spirit with no beginning and no end.

The circle symbol has that same quality. The space circle symbol has a dot in the middle which stands for consciousness. Like the structure of an atom, there is space between the dot and the outer circle. Space has neither colour nor shape and yet at the same time nothing exists without it. We should not forget that on the atomic level as well as in the universe itself space is the predominant element. Between the electrons and the nucleus of an atom there is an immense space.

This element brings us to the field of meditation, the experience of silence, the capacity to simply be. Space, sometimes called ether, fills everything between people, between objects. Moreover it allows what takes place between people. Sound is carried by the ether. The two opposed states of the element space are expression and suppression.

The Tibetans say: he who masters this element, knows the nature of spirit. He knows the essential and does not search on the outside in order to find the cause of his problems. Seeing them arise in space, he does not identify with them anymore (T.W. Rinpoche 2002). That is why in the Tibetan traditions of tantra and dzogchen space is considered to be the true centre.

The journey towards experiencing this element fully brings us mental space, stillness and opens up new horizons. Buddhists call it emptiness, the essence of spirit. This wisdom is held by many indigenous people who have kept alive this sacred link to their origins. 'Silence is the absolute balance of body, spirit and soul. People who can preserve this unity of being stay forever calm, untouched by the storms of existence' (Ohiyesa Indian, quoted in Tchendukua 2003)[3].

The body area that is especially associated with this element of space lies between the upper end of the chest bone and the bridge of the nose, so including the thyroid chakra, the ears, the mouth, the vocal chords and the point of silence at the bridge of the nose.

The Indian philosophical tradition notes that sound cannot travel in a void, so it is the space or ether element that provides the necessary medium for the movement of sound. The yogic tradition reminds us that it is this element that allows us to control our emotions. For when this element is active our consciousness moves away from its attachment to the sensual world. The active presence of this element is a prerequisite for any spiritual development or growth of mind.

---

3   Tchendukua is an association that helps the Kogi Indians in Columbia to restore their rituals and to get back some of their land.

To express space we need a good contact with the first four elements and the ability to transform the emotions associated with each chakra and each body zone. Our voice is an excellent witness to this process. Just as all our physical tensions are reflected in our neck, the thyroid energy centre will reflect all imbalances in the four lower chakras: root, hara, solar plexus and heart.

The qualities of space and silence are rare ingredients in western music. However, towards the end of the 1960s the space element was introduced more often. The recording studios began to use the effect of echo and reverberation more frequently, imitating the spacious sound quality found in some churches for instance. New Age music has been influenced by musicians who practise meditation and we may hear the quality of vast spaces in some electronic soundscapes and in synthesiser sound carpets. This development was paralleled by a renewed interest in Gregorian Chant, Tibetan singing bowls, gongs, overtone chanting, meditation music and by the creation of new kinds of instruments such as the monochord. It is probably not coincidental that it was in those years that the physical conquest of outer space was given so much attention. Let us remember the film 'Space Odyssey 2000'. The quality of space seems to have become universally more important since the 1960s.

WORKING SUGGESTIONS

Is the person able to listen to others playing? Can she comment on it? Is she able to communicate musically with another musician? If there is a lack of space in her music ask which other element(s) do attract our attention and start working with that element.

By emphasising the five elements in musical expression and by using sound paintings rather than melodies, all the participants in a workshop can *meet on the same level*, for in reality are we not all on the same level? In the context of real creativity, of any spiritual development, are we not always beginners in some way or other, whether young or old, musicians or non-musicians, mentally or physically more or less disabled? To be creative, to grow, demands of us a readiness to move into the unknown. Courage is needed and a playful or light-hearted approach – *as in music so in life*.

I worked in an institution for disabled adults for over two years giving weekly music workshops. Some of the staff and the majority of parents were resistant to this and could not see how music would do anything beneficial for these people. It was striking that it was members of the staff who would not participate in playing music. They probably felt more inhibited than the disabled participants themselves. The disabled adults, though, loved it and demonstrated how much these workshops had meant to them when at the final concert in front of parents and friends, every single disabled participant insisted on coming onto the stage to play. The music workshops had brought out their joy and was for some people a way to reduce the frustration of not being able to make themselves understood because of the lack of appropriate language.

In my courses I often let participants draw what they experience when someone else is playing. The presence or absence of certain elements, the specific forms that an element can take, are always as revealing for the participants as for those who are playing. The players realise how precisely feelings can be expressed and come to appreciate the wealth of information revealed in an improvisation. The five element approach gives us many keys to understand our psycho-energetic system, our emotions and thought structures, the tensions in our body, our beliefs and our deeper needs. It is always fascinating to see how much of our inner life is accurately reflected in our expression. Thus musicality, inspiration, creativity, luminosity in one's playing become accessible, understandable and are placed in a dynamic that everyone can learn to control.

When working with students, patients or clients it can be very helpful to be aware of when and how they engage with the five elements.

The five elements in Chinese and Tibetan traditions

In traditional Chinese medicine (TCM) one can find very old texts going back to Huang Di, the 'Yellow Emperor' in 600 BCE, that recommend the use of specific musical instruments because of their impact on one of the five phases of energy transformation, wood, fire, earth, metal and water (Husson 1973). Even though these five phases have similar names to the five elements with which I work, and are very often referred to as 'the five elements', they are used differently and do not mean exactly the same thing. They refer to five phases of energy when each element is continually being transformed into the next one in the cycle. 'Wood' in TCM is naturally tending towards 'fire' and 'fire' towards 'earth' and so forth.

This system differs from the five element system used in Ancient Greece, India, Tibet and developed by Paracelsus in Europe. In these systems the five elements represent five levels of densification of energy, going from the most subtle one ether to the most dense earth, the one that corresponds to the physical body. Nevertheless, TCM enables us to better understand the phenomenon of the five elements. There are numerous bridges of understanding between Chinese cosmogony and our own. Since we are all dealing with the same human condition this is hardly extraordinary.

TCM focuses more on the particular element's dynamic connection to the physical organs, the psychosomatic aspect as well as the energy meridians, while the psycho-energetic system focuses more on the different energy fields, especially on the etheric fields and the role of the chakras in the assimilation and distribution of energy. More research is needed to understand how the two systems are connected. Traditional Tibetan medicine has made that connection and has formulated a synthesis between three ancient systems of medicine, Indian, Chinese and Tibetan (T.W. Rinpoche 2002).

TCM suggests playing specific music instruments to activate each of the five phases of transformation. For the earth phase they suggest a clay pot into which one can blow to produce a deep sound, an ocarina for example. For the metal phase they suggest tubular bells, for the water phase drums, for the wood phase bamboo flutes and for fire instruments with silk strings are recommended although nowadays these would more likely be carbon fibre strings or gut stringed harps. For earth I sometimes use flowerpots with felt mallets and for water a large double-sided Nepalese frame drum. It is interesting to see how the TCM phase of earth corresponds in many ways to the element earth, in the psycho-energetic system, especially when it comes to the capacity for concentration. The water organs in TCM, bladder and kidneys, do nicely correspond to our hara chakra. TCM's wood includes the liver and is accordingly in the area influenced by the fire region in the solar plexus, while the TCM fire is linked to the heart towards which all energy moves naturally when transformed in the psycho-energetic fire area.

The five elements earth, water, fire, air and space are strongly present in Tibetan tradition, particularly in the bön tradition of pre-Buddhist times. They use an approach very similar to the psycho-energetic system in that their understanding is strongly influenced by observing how the elements behave in nature. The Tibetans' description of the qualities of the elements is very similar too. Tibetan tradition has also constructed bridges to the Indian ayurvedic tradition. Some Tibetan healing traditions use six chakras (T.W. Rinpoche 2002), others use five. Tenzin Wangyal Rinpoche's approach also makes a bridge to TCM by linking metal with air, wood with fire and TCM's fire with psycho-energetic's space. As often happens, this complementarity can inspire one to go deeper into the subject thus bringing one new understanding.

The Earth's Breath

Tonight it is warm and still with a rhythm that links
the trees, and the waves and the stars.
Boum, boum, boum,
deep in the earth is the pulse –
this is the earth's breath.
The sunrises in Australia,
kangaroo hopping through the bush,
the sound of a man screaming
in a police cell in Bangkok
a mother rocking her child through the night
Spanish fishermen catching sardines by lamplight.
Flashes of lives all over the world,
joy and pain, birth and death.
This is the movement that is snaking through the sky,
just above the surface of the earth…
eee, eeee, eeee, an infinity of sounds and images,
flashes of colour like a morse code in the sky,
an infinity of sounds in the airwaves.
Is this what Van Gogh could feel on starry nights
opening up to disappear into the whole?

Marie Perret, 1996

Chapter 3

Neuro-musical Thresholds

A long-term observation

Over many years I have been noting changes in a person's behaviour that seem to happen parallel to major breakthroughs in that person's musical expression. This can be observed more easily when someone is freely improvising which is often the best bridge linking 'inner reality' and expression. We can also detect such changes when someone is playing from memory or from musical scores. In my work as a music therapist in the CATTP of Corrèze, a therapeutic day clinic for children, I became aware of actual thresholds in their musical evolution. I am in charge of one of the clinic's several therapeutic workshops working with young autistic children, with psychotic children as well as with children with pervasive behavioural disorder. They are usually between four and eight years old, but sometimes come to us even younger. Most often I see only one child at a time for a weekly music therapy session that lasts half an hour. The child will come to music therapy for a period of two to four years, the average being thirty-two months totalling some fifty-eight sessions in music therapy. Usually the child will go to other workshops in the CATTP such as: painting or clay, video, fairy tales, TEACCH, psycho-drama, computer, wet room, psychomotoric therapy and speech therapy.

Seeing the same child over a period of several years allows us to observe phenomena that would be more difficult to detect in shorter periods of therapy. Obviously what we are looking for on a therapeutic level are significant and permanent changes in behaviour. Such changes apparently coincide sometimes with the crossing of what I call neuro-musical thresholds. I have so far detected seven major ones. During one year, in some two hundred sessions, I rarely witness more than half a dozen events like this. In my opinion this in itself stresses the importance of such thresholds.

The first time I became aware of the existence of thresholds which are difficult to cross, happened around the *passage from pulse to rhythm* (Perret 2003). I worked with 'Silver' for a whole year, without ever pushing him, but always trying to get him to grasp the difference between pulse and rhythm. 'Silver' was a boy of seven. I sang a rhythm or clapped it with my hands, I played it on an instrument or danced it. I tapped it on his back whenever he chose to lie flat on the large frame drum. Quite a few children love to lie on the large Tibetan drum. They do this quite spontaneously without being told to or shown that position. It is not unlikely that the skin of this large drum reminds them of lying on their mother's belly. One day one of them actually mentioned the word 'belly' when lying down on it (see the section on *water* in Chapter 2).

I realised the significance of these thresholds while observing other similar phenomena in the children's musical behaviour that were revealing hidden resistance. Whilst talking to colleagues and comparing what parents and school teachers had observed during the same period, I realised that the crossing of a major threshold could also show up in significant *changes in general behaviour* in other therapeutic ateliers, at school or at home. These thresholds seem to bear witness to neurological circuits in the brain that had not hitherto been activated well enough and as a result had temporarily lost their function. I talk more about this later on.

We can observe similar thresholds in the development of children's drawings. French psychoanalyst Geneviève Haag describes for instance the importance of the development of the vertical and horizontal axes, the shapes occupying the centre of the painting sheet, how the four corners are used, the appearance of returning loops, swaying lines, spirals and the appearance of the whole human body (Haag 1998).

Working therapeutically over a long period of time with someone who is obviously confronted with a major obstacle in their evolution is sometimes hard for the therapist to cope with. This is especially likely when working with a child who does not yet have any understandable language. Any compassionate therapist will of course tune into the child's energy field, her feelings and emotions, his mental state and energy structures. Often major obstacles include despair, suffering and painful emotions around rejection and failure. As therapists we can of course learn to protect ourselves from getting stuck in these conditions. In my own experience, though, when I have periods of three or four months where nothing seems to change for a child with whom I am working, the feeling of stuckness spreads to me as well as throughout the institution. This explains why the crossing over of a major threshold will be noticed by everyone and produces a general feeling of relief.

I have talked about the neuro-musical thresholds that I have noted with colleagues where I work and with others at international conferences. I have also contacted and chatted with researchers over the internet hoping to find reports by colleagues working on this subject. Not much seems to have been theorised about this as yet. (Research done in neuroscience that seems in particular to confirm the threshold of pulse/rhythm is considered later on in a discussion about the brain.)

I had been working for a little over two years with 'Rabbit' in music therapy. It was quite obvious that he could not get into any creative expression. He was stuck in a sort of aggressive attitude which regularly pushed him into a state of boredom. Both conditions are forms of self destructiveness. At some point I felt that he was ready to confront the threshold of creativity and to take a significant step. We had been building up a fairly good level of feeling contact and trust between us. I confronted him with my observations, talking to him like an adult. He was seven years old at that time. I insisted that he start to play music rather than just making noise. I told him that from now on I wanted him to be creative with music and to invent a song, a melody, anything. I added that I wanted him to enjoy himself and to be playful 'for God's sake!'. I had previously noticed that talking plainly to a child about what I was expecting from him and what I thought of his performance had produced significant effects. That is what happened with Rabbit.

On the other hand, if therapists only develop empathy towards their clients, we can fall into the trap of just adopting his own attitudes and beliefs about his inborn limitations. In thus becoming 'an accomplice' we contribute to limiting his growth process. From one day to the next Rabbit changed totally and crossed simultaneously three major thresholds: from pulse to rhythm, from boredom to creativity and he started using his voice to sing spontaneously. All the work we had been doing with him over months and years in various therapeutic workshops in the CATTP suddenly came to fruition.

Realising the importance of what was happening I went to talk to my colleagues asking them whether they had noticed significant changes with Rabbit since the end of September and the beginning of October. They had. It was quite noticeable to them that he was much less aggressive and had stopped talking about his obsessional subjects which were 'pots' and 'garbage'. He had become more affectionate and was increasingly expressing his emotions.

I remember a similar situation with 'Heron', who after three years of coming to music therapy had crossed the threshold of creativity. Again I had gone around talking to my colleagues asking what they had observed recently about Heron between the middle and end of January. In a painting session he had for the first time actually started to paint rather than remaining hidden under the table with the paints. In the computer atelier he had finally agreed to draw on a piece of paper at the end of the workshop, a task he had been asked to do after every session. He drew a human body, which is a well-known threshold in children's paintings.

My observations of thresholds have become clearer especially in the work I do with young children between three and eight years old. Apart from 'grasping the melodic organisation' of an instrument, which usually happens in childhood, the other major thresholds can be recognised in children as well as in adults with difficulties. I have come to understand three types of evolutionary thresholds in musical expression: *elementary thresholds* or themes of work, *permanent goals* or recurrent thresholds and the seven *major thresholds*. The crossing of any of these corresponds to a whole set of more or less important changes on different levels: emotional, cognitive, social, expressive, physical, sometimes on the level of the spoken language and very likely on a neurological level.

Elementary axes of work:

1. memorisation
2. fine motor movements
3. right/left balance
4. dance and movements

5. breathing motion (into a flute for instance)

6. voice, language and singing

7. trust and fun in participating.

Major neuro-musical thresholds:

1. concentration – element earth

2. experiencing the sound – element air

3. dynamism – element fire

4. rhythm – element water

5. creativity – element water and space

6. spontaneous singing – element space

7. melodic organisation – element air.

Permanent goals:

1. ability to harmonise and balance

2. ability to move someone and be radiant

3. expressing joy

4. creating intensity

5. taking part in creative musical communication

6. surrendering to inspirational expression

7. silence, receptivity, space and listening.

All of these thresholds are precise and playful axes of work. Nothing in spontaneous improvising is 'wrong' in itself. All musical expression can be evaluated in regard to musicality and reflection of inner phenomena. The major neuro-musical thresholds are the centre of our concept of evolutionary thresholds that concern mental and neuronal levels. Once crossed over they seem to belong to the definitive acquired 'skills' or rather functions, since it is not the musical activity that is important but the underlying function (emotional, mental, neuronal, behavioural). The elementary goals are axes of work in music therapy that are usually limited to work with children up to the age of eight. They can remain relevant though in working with people with special needs, originating at birth or later on, through accidents and other traumas. The permanent goals are thresholds but seem to require repeated crossings. They are never definitively acquired. Some people need to cross over them each time they want to express creatively. So each day, in each session they must get across the threshold again. Accordingly, they remain permanent goals in expression throughout life, but more specifically this is very likely to occur after the age of ten. Attaining these goals witnesses growth that may often become more important from adolescence onwards. These goals show vital needs of the soul and are signs of maturity.

What can we expect to be influencing us in working with these thresholds? Let us have a closer look at some recent discoveries in neuroscience.

Some notions about our brain

For some years I have felt compelled to try to understand the functioning of the brain and to read about neuroscience. It completes what psychology has been trying to make sense of. I have been fascinated by the research done by Hanna and Antonio Damasio from the University of Iowa in the United States and I was especially happy when I met the neurobiologist Colwyn Trevarthen, professor at the university of Edinburgh. For more than thirty years Colwyn has been observing the communication between mothers and their infants. His work has contributed to the understanding of the evolution of the brain that is so important in early life. Neuroscience, or science of the brain, has expanded rapidly in recent decades because of the development of ever stronger means of scanning the brain: MRI (magnetic resonance imagery), PET (positron emission tomography), EEG (electroencephalogram), TMS (transcranial magnetic stimulation). The results of these different scanning techniques show to what extent the brain is 'vacant' at birth.

At birth our brain seems to present an abundance of potential neuronal connections. These need to be activated through the infant's experiences within the first eighteen months of life. In a general way of speaking the ones most called into use will be strengthened, while the other ones may very well gradually deteriorate. The context in which the child is brought up will determine which part of the brain and therefore which neuronal connections will be used. This will determine his capacities or deficiencies later on in life.

Neuroscience has taught us a great deal about how the brain is formed and organised, but serious questions remain unanswered. Much effort has been devoted to detecting the cognitive aspects of the brain, perception and learning as well as the intellectual comprehension of the world. Research in this field, though, has suffered because for a long time the brain has been compared to a computer and its circuits. This is why up to now little research has been undertaken to understand the mechanisms of emotions and feelings and how they use and affect the brain. While we may know which parts of the brain are stimulated through this action or that emotion, we know very little about how a neuronal activity is actually translated into an image or a specific emotion, and vice versa, how an image and an emotion turn into a specific neuronal activity.

From birth our brain is the home for some thousand billion of *neurones*. Neurones are nerve cells that communicate between themselves through sending each other 'messages'. The bridge between two neurones, the interface, is called a *synapse* (Glaser 2000); only some of the synapses exist right from the start. Most of them are formed during the first few months after birth (Siegel 1998). The total number of synapses in any one brain will reach some 200,000 times the population of our planet (10^{15}) (Trevarthen 2003)! The volume of the human brain grows in its first year more than at any other time in our life (Gilles 1993, in Glaser 2000). At birth our brain weighs some 400g to reach 1000g at twelve months. This rapid growth continues until about the age of twenty-four months (Schore 1994, in Glaser 2000). Nevertheless recent studies show that the number of neurones and synapses continues to develop well beyond our first ten years (Quartz and Sejnowski 1997).

Neurones and their connections are created, expanded or deteriorate according to our experiences in life. While most of these links are selected according to their efficiency during the first eighteen months of life, the brain will remain malleable up to puberty and to a lesser degree after that (Trevarthen 2003). 'Neuronal constructivism', a more recent yet still quite minor current in brain research, believes that all learning influences activate the construction and development of neuronal circuits and does not just select the more favourable ones (Quartz and Sejnowski 1997).

During the first eighteen months of our life, the period of greatest plasticity for our brain, the influence of our environment is crucial. Already during our intra-uterine life the selection and production of neuronal links depends on the stimulus in our environment: touch, taste, mechanical stimulation, hearing, chemically through the placenta; I would personally also include the impressions and information we get through our feelings, through the spiritual and energy influences. Serious mental difficulties can result from a mother's severe malnutrition, from her abuse of alcohol or drugs, or indeed from major stress. Numerous observations seem to document that prolonged periods of stress, for instance through the death of a close member of the family, can have dramatic consequences. Death is not in itself the problem – it is a natural event and part of all life – but rather the cutting off of the feeling connection between the mother and the foetus, or the stress generated by the family, both of which leave the baby in a sort of feeling/emotional void that probably generates anxiety.

The psycho-energetic and transpersonal approaches generally underline that we are not passive victims of exterior circumstances, but rather that our soul, our inborn qualities, influence our beliefs and lead us to react in a very personal way to the environment, from the very beginning of our life in the womb. Very likely on a soul level we have chosen our environment and the events that we will meet in order to learn to deal with specific tasks and situations. Traditional psychology stemming from Freud's views has insisted that the source of all our troubles is the traumas in our childhood. According to the psycho-energetic approach though, there is a level of comprehension that lies beyond this conventional psychological layer. In all psycho-energetic approaches to therapy this vaster level of comprehension becomes essential. This by no means ignores the importance and understanding of the events of the first years of our lives.

In the formation of our brain there are more- and less-sensitive periods. These vary according to the specific part of the brain. Brain scientists seem to agree, however, that the prenatal period and the first year of life are crucial. The evolution of the frontal lobes, which are of paramount importance in the emotional functioning of human beings, lasts, as an especially sensitive period, until the second year of life. An emotional shock or neglect in the environment in this early period of life would manifest as an absence or lack of feeling interactions between parents and the infant. Evolutionary troubles such as autistic spectrum, evolutionary disharmonies and psychosis do very often have their origin in this period of life. That is why it is so important to detect them whenever possible before the age of two, better even before the age of one. After eighteen months, behaviour becomes much more settled and therefore harder to change and it becomes even more difficult after puberty. It is therefore of utmost importance to start a therapeutic work concerning these evolutionary troubles as soon as possible.

The organisation of the brain

The organisation of the brain is very complex. Most of the time, any activity – for instance moving a hand – requires participation by several centres in the brain. There are excellent books that expand on the subject (Damasio 1994). I prefer to concentrate on the functioning of the *two hemispheres* of the brain, which is of paramount significance in any musical expression.

The right hemisphere develops before birth slightly ahead of the left hemisphere. The processes involving the right hemisphere seem therefore to play a predominant role during pregnancy. During all early childhood, the right hemisphere is strongly influenced in its development by what happens between the baby and the mother or other partners. This part of the brain plays a role, amongst others, in the perception of shapes and all that will be visual–constructive tasks, as well as other important processes concerning non-verbal communication and emotional development. This hemisphere is, for example, very sensitive to the emotions carried by a voice, the feelings coming from another person as well as the quality of expression in a song or in instrumental music. That is the reason why music therapy, or playing music in general, can be important in working with this crucial early childhood period, since both essentially operate in a non-verbal way. Music though reaches far beyond the pre- and non-verbal (Trevarthen and Malloch 2000). This is discussed later on.

It is also in the right hemisphere that we find our capacities concerning bodily sensations and the feeling awareness of oneself. The left hemisphere is more concerned with our logical faculties and reasoning. Each hemisphere corresponds to a different way of viewing the world, two distinct ways of functioning. Both are necessary. It remains a question why nature has provided us with two such hemispheres. Why do we not have a single 'unitary brain'?

Table 3.1 Left and right hemispheres of the brain

Left hemisphere of the brain	Right hemisphere of the brain
Corresponding to right side of body	Corresponding to left side of body
Male principle	Female principle
Expression, performance	Receptivity
Intellect and linear analysis	Innovation, intuition, inspiration
Cause-and-effect relationship	Search for sense
Sequential treatment	Global treatment and view (atmosphere)
Sense of quantity	Sense of quality
Material level	Energy and spiritual level
Grammar, vocabulary	Poetic value of words and phrases
Semantic	Perception of shapes and forms
	Visual–constructive tasks
	Perception of own body, emotions and feelings
	Awareness of self and of imagination
In music	*In music*
Score reading, theory of music	Free improvisation, sound paintings
Instrumental technique	Timbre, musicality
Lexical knowledge	Quality of sound
Logical side of the structure of a musical mode or scale, sequence of a melody or rhythmic cell	Ambience for instance of a musical mode or of a musical scale
Media aspect of music	

The feeling aspect of music is essentially linked to the right hemisphere, feeling, musicality, imaginary aspects, deeper needs, quality of sound, overall sense, even if obviously in our 'western' societies musical education has for quite some time stressed the importance of the intellectual approach to music. Accordingly, the left hemisphere of the brain is more engaged for writing music, score-reading, stressing the importance of technical aspects in learning, the structure of a composition, virtuosity, speed of playing, 'mistakes' in playing, information concerning biographical data of a composer or musician, etc. In music therapy as well as in music education we can reinforce the neglected right-brain approach and activate in this right-brain inter-neuronal connections for someone who has not had the opportunity to grow up in an environment favourable to a harmonious evolution (Glaser 2000).

In the young child, the right hemisphere of the brain remains dominant during the first three years of life. It will be playing an important role in the non-verbal aspects of language (the tone in one's voice, movements of arms and hands linked to speech), facial expression of emotions, perception of emotion, regulation of the autonomous nervous system, perception of body sensations and the understanding of social situations, including being able to imagine oneself in the role of the other partner, that is being able to feel what the other one might think and feel (Siegel 1998).

The left hemisphere will become more important during the emergence of language. It will be dominant for all semantic aspects – the logic and the organisation – of language *and* rhythms as well as musical narration. This hemisphere plays a major role in constructing cause-and-effect relations and linear analysis, that is, intellectual logic.

Neuroscience and psycho-energetic approach

In our present understanding neurones not only have an influence on the physical links between brain and body and vice versa, but they will also have an effect on the functioning of our mental energy field and vice versa. The mental energy field's role is to control other levels of energy: the emotional field, the etheric and the subconscious memory stored there, as well as on the functioning of the various energy centres, chakras, with their respective specific emotional and spiritual tasks. Physical, neuronal and energetic aspects are intricately linked. There remains the task to create bridges of understanding between neuroscience, trans-personal psychology and the understanding of the energy fields that are part of our make-up.

It seems obvious to me that an accumulation of stress felt in a specific area of the mental energy field, exterior to the skull and brain, does have an immediate influence on the structures of the brain next to it and vice versa. Every emotional shock influences our mental energy field and the selection of neuronal links to be constructed, reinforced or to be abandoned in the brain. Entire zones like the frontal lobes can become underdeveloped if the emotional life of the young child is significantly disturbed. Several zones of the brain are very sensitive to the feeling quality of contact between parents and child, even before birth. Numerous scientific research results confirm this. Thus specific faculties will be only partially developed if his life's experience makes the infant withdraw into particular behavioural patterns, that will in turn bring about the neglect of other more optimal patterns that would lead to a more balanced life.

The emotional experience is absolutely essential for our development. The American neuroscientist Damasio has shown that any person cut off from his bodily sensations, say after a cerebral lesion due to an accident, stroke or operation, will find himself also cut off from his emotions (Damasio 1994). The person will consequently have only partial access, or none at all, to his feelings. This will lead to an incapacity to take new decisions in life, decisions that would be out of the ordinary routine. The reason for this is that he will no longer have the means to evaluate the consequences of alternatives, thus becoming unable to choose reasonably between them.

On a therapeutic level, we believe it to be possible to find activities that influence directly the neuronal paths that lack stimulation or that can create new ones. Children in the autistic spectrum are inclined to close themselves off from the perception and expression of their emotions. This is why they limit their communication with others and lock themselves into their own world. This autistic behaviour is narrowly linked to the use of specific neuronal paths and parts of the brain. Therapeutic work concentrates on activating other paths, by suggesting precise activities that the child or adult may tend to avoid. We need to find a playful approach – not threatening – that proves to be efficient as well. It seems that the practice of specific musical tasks would do exactly this: activating precise parts or paths of the brain that are needed by someone to catch up with a more common human evolution.

We know for instance that the sequential treatment of language happens at the very same place in the brain as the sequential treatment of rhythms (in the area of Broca, Brodmann Area (BA) 44 and 6; Platel *et al.* 1997) and that the area of the brain concerned with our hand movements lies next to it. Therefore, there is a very strong likelihood that working with rhythms in a specific way will lessen a person's linguistic difficulties. That is why I coined the term 'neuro-musical thresholds'. The work we did at the CATTP with 'Flamingo', a six-year-old boy, seems to confirm that the clear improvement in the sequential construction of his language was significantly helped by the previous eight months of rigorous work memorising and reproducing rhythmical and melodic cells on the xylophone and a hand drum.

I do not completely agree with a number of neuroscientists who claim that emotions, thoughts, memories, perceptions, intentions, beliefs and attitudes are all part of our mental states and should therefore be manifested in our brain (Siegel 1998). In my observation the frequency in the mental energy field is very much higher than the frequency in the emotional energy field. These are two distinct phenomena. I believe that all the phenomena listed above pass in the first place not through the brain but through the physical body. I am convinced, though, that for any therapeutic work with sound and music to be of lasting effect, it needs to be combined with a movement in consciousness, that is to say with a new awareness. Awareness is a mental process that includes both hemispheres of the brain. In my work I place emphasis on improving contact with all the parts of the body. Each part has links to specific emotions, memories and thought structures. Therefore it is only when we improve the contact to certain areas of the body that we can successfully integrate hidden, or subconscious, aspects that otherwise would be likely to lead their 'own life' beyond our conscious control, thus creating havoc in our emotional and mental lives as well as having in the long run possible adverse consequences for our health.

Whatever the mechanisms underlying the emotions may be, the body is their main stage either directly or through their representations in the somato-sensorial structures of the brain (Damasio 1999). Taking these thoughts a step further I suggest that certain types of emotion have a link to more specific parts of the body (see Chapter 2). My research, as well as the work of colleagues (Gamborg 1998; Perret 1997) leads me to believe that our emotions, just as much as our subconscious memory, are actually not part of the mental even if they obviously do have a strong impact on it. The work of David Boadella, director of the Biosynthesis Institute in Switzerland, is leading in the same direction (Boadella 1987). In his book he underlines how much the zones of our body linked to the chakras correspond to the zones of psychophysical blockages revealed by the work of Wilhelm Reich (see Table 2.1).

It would be very interesting to deepen our understanding of the link that very likely exists between zones of energy restriction that we can sense in the mental aura and the activity in the zones of the brain next to where the restriction shows up. There is much evidence suggesting that the neurones of the brain react not only to impulses or movements of energy from inside the body but also to movements in the mental energy field, exterior to the body. Let us have a closer look as to why music could be an efficient tool in this work.

Biological roots of musicality

During the three months before birth, the unborn child is able to use a fully developed auditory system. He can hear and learn to recognise rhythms as well as his mother's voice. Scientists such as Trevarthen show us how the biological roots of our musicality reach back to a time before our birth. In our mother's womb we move in an ocean of sound that links us with the outside world. We can hear the voice of our mother and of other people too. We live with the rhythms of our two hearts, of our mother's breathing, the noises of her digestion, the rhythmical move-ments when she walks or moves her arms, the rhythms and noises of day and night.

From the very first moments after birth the newly-born experiences a 'musical communication' using sounds, melodies, the feeling of voices, the nuances in the timbre and the rhythms that very much resemble a musical improvisation. The rituals in communication are present from the start, becoming more important as the days go by, forming the biological and social bases of our musicality. In those first communications we can already observe musical laws at work, like the rhythm ruling the succes-sion of 'questions' and 'answers', the melodic line of a phrase, synchronic movements of the tiny fingers, hands, arms and legs of the new-born that go with the communication (Trevarthen and Aitken 2001). Newly-born babies are attracted by any songs and music and react with much interest and manifestations of joy. After three months the 'proto-conversations' give way to games involving the body, clapping hands, tickles, games of hide-and-seek and children's songs. Many of these activities are governed strongly by rhythm, with a steady phrasing, highly predictable repetitions and, at the end, a resolution of the emotional energy

(Trevarthen and Aitken 2001). When a baby approaches the age of six weeks we can observe that the communication between baby and parents often follows an *adagio* beat (70 pulses per minute) similar to the alternating sequence of 'questions' and 'answers'. One or two months later, during more animated moments, the rhythm of the vocal games accelerates to become an *andante* (90 pulses per minute) or even *moderato* (120/min.). In the six months following birth more changes happen in the cellular structure of the brain than in any other period of our development.

The faculty of the infant to recognise from very early on a multitude of musical elements in the voice of his mother, timbre, crescendo, rhythm, slowing down, the qualities of fire, earth, air, etc., allows him to fine-tune his reactions to changes in mood, tiredness, joy, astonishment, worry or dissimulation, to reassure himself and to confirm that the mother has understood the signals concerning his needs. The baby does not, however, simply react to the mother's signals. She, in turn, responds to the rhythms and emotional content of the infant's expression, in an interactive improvisation: a duo. The two beings use all the registers of vocal expression as well as movements, body, hands, face to make 'music' together. The mother is very aware of the musicality in the expression of the baby while communicating with him (Trevarthen and Aitken 2001).

Trevarthen is convinced that music as such, and in a larger sense 'active musicality' is the origin of the activation of states of consciousness as well as of the *development of intelligence*, through the combination of an investigative curiosity and communication (Trevarthen 2000a). He describes what he considers to be the psycho-biological roots of musicality. According to his research and the work of his colleagues, biological evidence is undeniable, our sense of communication, our ways of moving the body, follow the laws of harmony, the laws of music. Spoken language, our physical movements, as well as music itself are based on rhythms in the brain and rhythms originating in the melodic urges of our emotions. He is convinced that the parameters of musicality are determined in the brain or are acquired from birth and are necessary for human development. He describes brilliantly the psycho-biological roots of musicality, but we need also to understand more about its psycho-energetic roots.

The human being is not just 'biological' or 'brain'. While Trevarthen knows this, he concentrates his research on the processes of our consciousness and how these can be found operating in the brain or in the communication between mother and babies. Even if powerful scanners will probably always detect movement in the brain when a person is being emotional or thinking, remembering or perceiving the outside world, there remains a number of unanswered questions.

While neuroscience has brought about spectacular progress in understanding the functioning of the brain, of emotions and physical movements, of the subconscious movements of our body, breathing, digestion, movement of the blood stream or endocrine glands, there remain numerous questions on the origin and the localisation of phenomena such as thought, consciousness, intuition and inspiration. While nowadays we are able to tell which centres of the brain and which parts of the body participate in any emotion, movement or musical expression, we still do not know what happens between the activation of specific neurones and the production of an actual image, a melody, a visual–auditory full-sense memory or an inspiration, and vice versa we do not know how an inspiration is translated into an activation of neuronal circuits in the brain. Damasio may describe consciousness as the feeling of a feeling and point at the place in the brain where this is registered, but he comes to the conclusion that there are a number of questions that he cannot answer: of what are feelings made? Of what are they the expression? How far can we actually explore them (Damasio 1999)?

Pathologies and evolutionary disharmonies

At the CATTP I work with young children who show evolutionary disharmonies or pervasive developmental disorders, some being in the autistic spectrum. Others display shades of neurosis or even psychosis. A child with evolutionary disharmonies may nevertheless have several capacities that have evolved normally, for instance, perception and physical evolution while other features may show a delayed development, for example speech or affective capacities. These disharmonies can take on a multitude of variations and involve different areas – behavioural or neuronal – which in every case demand a specific pedagogic and therapeutic approach.

While I have seldom felt the urge to study long books on mental pathologies, I have recently read with great interest the works of Pierre Delion (1997) and Geneviève Haag (1998). I have not previously felt like reading at great length about pathologies partly because I believe them to be mainly of medical concern. In music therapy I am presented with individuals whose particular differences are far more important than any medical label that may try to define any group of patients with similar problems. My major objective is to help each person access their innermost being. I am convinced that any real therapeutic action in the field of the psyche needs to be rooted in compassion, respect and a contact with the healthy essence of the being, his innate qualities, his abilities that come with him at birth, his spiritual capital, so to say. It is this contact that needs above all to be reinforced and encouraged. Any harmonising practice needs to be rooted in this level, a level that is never affected by any deficiency or hurt of any kind. It is in fact the only possible starting point from where a harmonisation and a healing can take place.

To know that a child was classified autistic, psychotic or anything else, has never helped me to find the door to his or her essence. Any one child suffering from autistic troubles, for instance, will always be extraordinarily different from another autistic child. Recently, professionals prefer to speak of an 'autistic spectrum' thereby admitting that there are probably just as many variations of autism as there are children suffering from it. The difference between two autistic children I have worked with has always been for me as vast as the difference between two patients with different pathologies. Consequently, knowing the medical dossier of a patient has very rarely helped me in my work. With one child – not classified autistic – I found the doorway to his essence was through his sense of humour which was still intact despite all his difficulties. With another child – one classified autistic this time – I had to follow the track of humour through the swift contacts of our hands on the large frame drum placed between us. With yet another autistic child, I shall call him 'Semaphore', I had to let him guide me during the sessions towards the door to his essence. With 'Feather' I had to wait for two years before finding the door. I will tell her story later on. It turned out that it was 'dancing' that she had come to music therapy for and it was dancing that made her happy. Fortunately, thanks to music and all the wonderful instruments we have in the music therapy atelier, we would often have had moments of laughter and warm feeling contact between us before we found the door. This helps us both not to 'lose each other out of sight'.

The 'doorway' that allows a deeper energy flow to circulate between us is unique to each relationship. All preconceived ideas about it tend to conceal it. It is important to leave behind all knowledge and experience, to put oneself on an equal level with whomsoever one is working, which we truly are anyway, and be fully present just person-to-person, remaining patient until the access is given.

Sound and autism

Many autistic children do have a hypersensitivity to sound in general and certain sounds in particular. Music therapy is thus a very special means to work with them. Several questions come forward as to why someone has this particular interest in or resistance to sound. The roots could come from the pre-birth period, when the unborn infant may have been flooded with stressful sounds coming from outside. These sounds may have been linked to situations when strong emotions were being expressed: fights, shouting, smashing of doors, screams, cries, but also the sound of sirens or any other sound provoking fear in the mother might be involved. It is possible that any painful interruption of the mother's attention towards the foetus caused by a stressful circumstance such as a death, illness or absence of the partner, could have created worry in the child. He may have wondered what was happening, why his mother was not 'there' for him anymore. He would reach out with the one sense that was operating very well after the fifth month in the womb, that is, his hearing.

These are just hypotheses. We can only guess that the foetus has been exposed to a traumatism linked to a disturbing impact that has torn open the usually safe *envelope of sound*, which is usually a range of well-known rhythms of the mother's heart – slower at night, faster moving in the daytime, even faster when she is hurrying, or the rhythms of her digestive system. The unborn child would perhaps experience a combination of hearing, the predominant sense in this intra-uterine phase, and the sensation of a strong unpleasant emotion. The child coming to music therapy may then be looking to repair the ruptured 'envelope of sound' or to work therapeutically on it. We still know rather little about the origins of autism. We know that they very likely occur during the first eighteen months of life, including the pre-birth period, and that sound is a very efficient means to act upon these pre-verbal spaces.

Frances Tustin, in her book *Autism and Protection* (1990), describes in an impressive way how these prolonged interruptions of attention on the part of the adult carer create 'holes' that are so painful for the toddler, that he ends up shutting himself off from their memory, the connected emotions, the representation of the parent, his imagination, to be left only with trusting his sense of touch.

> For him, only what is tangible and physically present will trigger excitement. Memories, images, phantasms, and thoughts are intangible. The excessive importance attached to permanent physical contact inhibits any normal development of the mental life. With inadequate memories and images, the imaginary is impaired. And the imaginary level is essential for playing. (Tustin 1990)

Music therapy can recreate the broken bridge between the world of touch and the imaginary. I am again and again impressed when I see to what degree the young children with autism, aged only three to eight years old, with whom I am working in music therapy can let themselves be fascinated by the sounds they produce on the instruments. They feel like 'fish in water' and are obviously 'in their element'. They explore mostly in their own way, autonomously, taking the lead themselves, using me as a containing presence that will eventually help them to weave and restore the delicate web that makes up communication.

It is very interesting to note that most autistic children pass through a phase where they are afraid of any *sound of running water* – read for this the psycho-energetic importance of the element water and its link to the belly area. At the same time they feel a fascination for the sound of water and subconsciously seem to know that it has a healing power for them. They will pull the flush in the lavatory a hundred times watching the water disappear. 'Whirlwind' had the intelligence to always find the sounds he needed in the music atelier. For almost a year for some time in every session he used to walk around with the rainstick to his ear, turning it upside down again and again just to hear the running of its 'water'. He finally got rid of this obsession, even if once in a while he had to do it again and probably would continue to do this. We, too, are fascinated by the sound of rain, a brook or the waves breaking at the sea shore. Very likely this is not by chance, since it would correspond to a need linked to our hara (water), to a feeling maybe that we need more fluency, more vitality and to this end must unblock an obstruction and restore some flow (see Chapter 2).

> 'Whirlwind' had an intense encounter with the monochord. This is a string instrument with some forty-five long metal strings tuned to one note. During the first sessions he would scream when coming into the room, as if someone was about to torture him. Fortunately this phase was soon over. Then he would occasionally approach the instrument on all fours, briefly touch it and withdraw rapidly as if hit by lightning. Some months later he wanted to listen to its sound continuously. Either he would give me a sign that he wanted me to sound it or every two minutes he would briefly interrupt his activity at the other end of the room to come over and strike its strings. After a year he seemed to have domesticated it. Then, three month before his leaving the CATTP, during my absence he managed to damage it seriously by throwing a clay flowerpot on it. I use flowerpots as a lithophone. His relationship with the monochord will remain something of a mystery, even if we can speculate that for him it represented a sort of secure and mothering sound envelope. The monochord provides the possibility of experiencing the harmonic notes beautifully. It also echoes any sound in the room by means of resonance.

If my hypothesis is correct, the crossing over of one of the major thresholds should have direct consequences on the patient's general behaviour. The crossing of a neuro–musical threshold should in a significant and durable way activate or restore some areas of the brain. Relying on our comprehension of the psycho-energetic links we would expect changes to happen in specific areas such as the person's relation to his physical body, to the corresponding emotions, to expression. All changes in the lower four main energy centres or chakras would bring about a change in the thyroid chakra, which would show up in the person's freer expression and so there would be less suppression. Changes in the voice might well occur, sometimes resulting in someone being able to sing spontaneously. An evolution towards a truer and direct expression of emotions might be observed. This would diminish activities that had been used to cover up painful emotions. A better control of emotions through the mental level, not only the intellectual left side of the brain, and possibly a greater influx of spiritual energy might arise: joy, feeling more secure and calmer, amongst other signs.

The elementary thresholds: axes of work in childhood

Numerous non-logical thresholds can be observed in musical expression. They can become obstacles in the mastering of a musical instrument, the understanding of a precise musical phenomenon, the radiance of a performance or the musicality of the musician. Often repeating the passage may help to overcome the obstacle, whereas others may prove more tenacious. Then, if the necessary understanding of the inner processes involved is missing, a teacher or therapist or indeed the person himself could be tempted to force the issue. That is when some damage may be caused to oneself or the other, which is actually the same thing. In the best of cases this incident might be soon forgotten, at worst it will lead someone to abandon the playing of music altogether. Many patients have told me their particular version of this very same story. Understanding the different levels involved in playing music allows us to avoid that and gives us tools to guide the patient and pupil towards a greater expansion and musicality.

I remember asking one of my students, I believe she was in the sixth year of studying music with me, to play 'water'. We had decided that it was time to work with improvisation. I could see that she felt blocked about the task. Some painful minutes followed. Then she started to cry silently. This made me say with a smile that she probably was not aware how close she had got to expressing this very theme of 'water' through shedding tears. When she tried anew, some moments later, she managed beautifully. The intellect has got to abdicate before such a task and the right side of the brain may take over for a length of time. After that there are but a few criteria left that allow us to understand if a person actually is playing 'water' in any of its multiple forms. Everyone will succeed more or less. Basically the player will know whether the expression did correspond to the feeling of 'water' or whether it remained an abstract thought while our intellect actually remained in control and messed it all up.

Let us look at a number of elementary thresholds that can be worked on. Normally, as with the major thresholds, once these elementary thresholds are crossed they are no longer a problem. They are important axes of work in music education and music therapy. We would of course also find these thresholds in this or a similar form outside music, at school, in other therapeutic ateliers or at home. All of them can be worked with in music and will need our full attention. Difficulties in crossing over any threshold may hide inner obstacles, sometimes inborn, sometimes emotional, sometimes neuronal, sometimes all three of them.

Memorisation

While memorising seems mainly to be a problem of the left brain, of our intellect, that is, there is much evidence that co-operation with the right brain will greatly help memory. Frequently, educational programmes suggest the simultaneous use of baroque music, Mozart, or other slow music to help someone memorise something. There are different types of memorising. Sequential memory is a phenomenon of the left-hand side of the brain, the same as for language. This necessitates remembering the sequence of events like words, rhythmical cells, melodies, a road to take, a series of numbers. The memorising of timbre, atmospheres of musical modes, the quality of intervals, the overall ambience of a place or tune are possibly more of a task for the right side of the brain.

Fine motor movements

We find the importance of fine movement capacity underlined in professor Hubert Montagner's work on the *cinq compétences socles* or 'five basic competences' that make out the structured and directed organisation of movement. In playing musical instruments you would be able to work practically on all aspects of the fine movement capacity as well as the right/left hand co-ordination.

Right/left balance

Neuroscience has been studying this subject for years. Without getting into the debate on true and false left-handers or right-handers we know that in the brain the area which deals with the hands' movements lies right beside the important language centre. Due to the crossing over of the nerves, the left hand, in fact all the left side of the body, is linked to the right hemisphere of the brain and vice versa. The left hand has, therefore, generally speaking, a special link with our female, intuitive and receptive aspect while the right hand on a deeper level is more strongly connected to the male, analytical, outgoing side.

Co-ordination of both hands can be trained on several music instruments. One is the hand drum, when it is large enough to allow both hands to play at the same time. You can recognise such a lot just by noticing how someone uses her hands on a drum. A task that asks for more skill is playing two notes at the same time on the xylophone, leaving one note out between them. This playing of thirds, while transposing them up and down the scale, asks for significant co-ordination and subsequently is quite useful for training the left-right-hand balance.

Dance and movements

Not everyone finds it easy to express herself through dancing while enjoying herself at the same time. But for anyone having this access dance can bring a great sense of liberation. Some may find it to be the way to their deepest expression and greatest joy.

This was true for 'Feather'. She had been coming to music therapy for over two years during which time I had tried everything that crossed my mind to find what could grab her and make her invest herself in music therapy, except dance. For a while I let her share the atelier with another child. But I quickly had to give this up because she needed all my attention if we were to do some real therapeutic work together. Either I would give her all my attention and leave out the other child or sooner or later I would have to scold her because she tried to get my undivided attention all the time. This would send her into a depressive withdrawal which was unacceptable in a therapeutic workshop. Her story is recounted in Chapter 1.

The capacity of being able to synchronise a pulse with a song or some music, happens in parallel to this threshold of dance.

Breathing motion (into a flute for instance)

Recently I was astonished to observe that blowing, into a flute for instance, can be a really difficult thing to do for some of the children who come to our day clinic.

Voice, language and singing

It is rare to find a child coming to the CATTP who does not find it difficult to sing. Either he finds it difficult to sing audibly or impossible to sing at the same time as banging a drum, for example.

Trust and fun in participating

In any therapeutic relationship establishing a trusting connection is essential. With a child who has been mistreated this can take some time to achieve. Music therapy fortunately offers a number of playful activities that can help a child take the first steps.

Working in music with the five elements will introduce us to other phenomena that reveal the characteristics of a threshold. When I ask someone to play the *mountain*, she will have to contact an inner quality linked to an inner strength, a male aspect, a feeling of strong anchoring and a sense of individuality. Once we have seen that the patient's or student's musical expression is truly reflecting his or her feelings and reality we can then observe how the qualities of *mountain* actually are expressed in their play, singing or dancing. If the above mentioned qualities are not present or are only partially present in their expression, the feeling of *mountain* will reflect this. Very likely this *mountain* quality will be missing in any other musical interpretation and of course in their everyday life as well. (See Chapter 2 for more details.)

It is very likely that there are a number of other thresholds, such as becoming aware of a musical interval. A musical expression that truly reflects inner feelings will, like any musical element or quality, potentially expose the characteristics of a neuro-musical threshold. Thereafter, illogical obstacles in musical expression, or expression in general, start making sense.

The major neuro-musical thresholds

My research on these thresholds is in an ongoing process and is still somewhat in its infancy, in spite of the fact that I have been collecting evidence for them for a number of years. Consequently, the list of neuro-musical thresholds is not complete and probably never will be. Research and, I hope, exchanges amongst readers, scientists and music therapists need to focus on significant changes which happen in parallel to someone crossing over a threshold. We can clearly distinguish as far as the more important or major thresholds which concern the personal development of a person. For the time being I have detected seven of them. The first one is not detectable in music alone of course. In fact all of them can be observed in our general expression, in our movements, in our way of talking, in the sound of our voice. They reflect our whole being.

If the major thresholds often relate to working with children it is because their brain has yet to fully develop, which development continues at least until puberty. This does not mean that we cannot work with adults on issues concerning the brain. In normal circumstances, however, they would already have crossed these thresholds – except for the first one that asks for a permanent effort. When working with adults I would, therefore, be more likely to use the five elements: for example asking them to play an element such as *water, a large river* or a *mountain,* having carefully chosen the aspect of their psycho-energetic make-up on which they need to focus. I would also include the work on the seven permanent thresholds (see further on in this chapter).

Let us go through the major thresholds in the most naturally occurring sequence. For instance, the capacity to concentrate is funda-mental to all therapeutic work. It brings about the necessary trust and security.

There is much evidence that each one of these major thresholds is more specifically linked to a zone of the body with its set of emotions and thought structures (Boadella 1987; Gamborg 1998; Perret 1997; Perret 2001; Satyasangananda 2000).

Getting access to concentration – earth

It is obvious that we cannot get very far in music therapy if the patient cannot concentrate and settle down. This incapacity is a sign of a lack of contact with one's earth. By the way, traditional Chinese medicine links the same symptoms to their energy phase of earth. Contacting the earth or 'grounding' is fundamental. Grounding is narrowly associated with being in one's body, being able to centre one's attention on an object or a precise activity, not getting quickly distracted, not having one's thoughts wandering off in all directions. Being able to concentrate shows the capacity to 'face up' to somebody or something. This leads to being responsible – able to respond as an individual and to make choices. I have already mentioned Damasio's findings on the importance of being able to experience one's body and emotions in order to be able to make new decisions (see above, the section on 'Neuroscience and psycho-energetic approach' p.98).

In traditional Chinese medicine the capacity to concentrate is linked to the stomach and the spleen. We know that the impact of emotions coming from other people penetrate our system precisely there, in the area of the solar plexus chakra. It is in this zone, with the diaphragm's help, that we would tend to block our energy flow so as not to feel our emotions. This leads to a superficial breathing that avoids any abdominal breathing. We then get cut off from our 'emotional sounding board' which is the belly area. The emotions then go straight into the subconscious (see the water area of the psycho-energetic system), where they remain out of reach for our consciousness. This underlines the importance of concentration. Lack of concentration very often reveals a lack of contact with the belly area, the legs and suppressed emotions. Grounding remains a constant challenge for everyone. There are simple exercises that can help grounding (Perret 1997).

It may be necessary to limit the number of instruments available in music therapy to help concentration and to counteract distraction, otherwise the lower mental level takes over. Then the patient is 'speedy' and cannot settle or calm down. In this state of mind the person will have gone through all the instruments in five minutes and will want to leave. When this happens the therapist will have firmly to structure the session (structure = earth), telling him to stay working on the drum together or keeping him from wanting to change the instruments into non-musical objects when influenced by his restless fantasy.

Deep slow breathing into the belly area, foot massage, putting bands of bells on the ankles and having the child stamp his feet on the ground while dancing would help to bring the energy down from the head area to the legs and feet. In this phase children often spontaneously want to take off their socks and even to put their feet on the drum while sitting on the floor. It is important to establish a safe and secure atmosphere for them where they feel accepted and never to be abrupt with them. This process of grounding will take time but cannot be avoided. This threshold of concentration is so fundamentally important that I could also have included it with the elementary axes of work.

During the course of writing this book, the following happened:

After some eight months of working with 'Semaphore' in music therapy we had not gone very far in terms of musical communication. Semaphore was seven years old and suffering from severe autism. Though he was not talking at all, he would understand almost every word I said. When I called to him in the garden to come to music therapy he would dash out from behind a bush and run to get his pictogram 'music'. Then he would rush down the stairs to the music room.

Semaphore had severe difficulties in concentration and in staying with one instrument. I could hardly show him anything. He always insisted on doing everything by himself, following his own track in his own way, very much as 'Whirlwind' had done before him. After this initial period of eight months, he crossed the threshold of concentration and stepped into the experience of sound. We had a series of sessions where he was clearly more concentrated and a lot calmer. Suddenly he could stay four or five minutes playing on the big drum. One of the only moments of communication at that time was around this drum. Our hands would come closer and closer while playing until – a moment anticipated by Semaphore – I would flap my hands onto his. He would smile briefly but happily and go on to something else. Towards the end of the session he would often lie down peacefully as if saying: 'Go on, I don't mind at all!' I would continue to play and sing. After one of these first 'successful' sessions I was talking with a colleague, when Semaphore arrived. He took my hand and placed it onto his heart, meaning that the session had made him really happy. This gesture of his moved me deeply.

This child has considerably challenged my efforts to theorise. At that time, on a musical level not much was happening with Semaphore during music therapy. He could not play any rhythms. He would not construct anything tangible. His creative efforts had to be divined with much effort since his playing on any instrument did not exceed twenty seconds. We had hardly any musical communication in the strict sense of the word. He would take the beater out of my hand when he wanted me to stop playing or put one into my hand if he wanted me to play, but our musical exchange seemed to stop there. Consequently, in the session I describe above, what had been so different and therapeutically valuable? Was it that his concentration improved significantly after he had managed to play with the large drum for a much longer period? For the first time he did not want to leave the atelier at the end of the session, whereas usually he had done his tour of the instruments in ten to fifteen minutes. There had also been the long moment towards the end of the session when lying on the floor he looked at me tenderly smiling while I continued singing and playing the guitar.

What had happened, since musically there had not been any significant progress? Or is the essential part of the therapeutic encounter not happening on a musical level at all? If that is the case, what is the role of a *music* therapist in all this?

In Semaphore's general behaviour we could clearly notice that along with his new capacity to show feelings and tenderness, he now had moments where he literally exploded with pain, moving through major emotional crises which were probably linked to an overwhelming sense of shame, of being useless and failing to make himself properly understood. Again I remembered 'Whirlwind' who had gone through a similar phase of intense emotions. This is obviously a necessary step to re-own one's emotions and it is thus a hopeful sign. As Damasio describes (1994), feelings come after one has renewed contact with feeling emotions, which happens parallel with getting one's body awareness back, especially with the lower part of the body. This phenomenon is well known amongst body therapists and in the literature on autism.

Some three weeks after these sessions Semaphore surprised me by playing on the xylophone four times in a row a well-known French song 'Au claire de la lune'. He played it rhythmically correctly by using a beat for every note though without being able to play the melody itself. He

had not yet passed over the threshold of 'grasping the melodic organisation' of the instrument. In seven years of work at the CATTP children's
day clinic no other child had ever gone so far! I had shown him the
melody once or twice some four weeks before without him showing any
sign that he had memorised it. Children often reveal what they have
learned after some delay.

Getting access to the experience of sound – air

This is a door that must be walked through if the person wants to be able
to enjoy the world of sound and music, which is in many ways 'the world'
in general. Accessing the experience of sound creates a link between concentration and feeling. This is an experience connected to the right hemisphere of the brain. You will know that someone is getting into the experience of sound by the sense of wonder that takes hold of her. I am
convinced that the experience of sound opens us up to the feeling content
in communication, the messages between the lines and behind the words.
In French there is a saying: 'C'est le *ton* qui fait la musique!' – The essential
part of music lies in the quality of the sound.

My belief is that it is of paramount importance in music therapy to
offer instruments that are a sound event in themselves. The quality level
of instruments has often proven to be very useful. It is a waste of money to
want to do music (-therapy) on 'cheap' instruments. Switzerland and
Germany have been extremely innovative in the past twenty years by
creating a whole range of new therapeutic instruments (see Appendix 1).

The experience of sound needs to move through a phase of relaxation, of receptivity and listening of course, but the kind of listening
linked to feelings and the female side in us. The entrance door may very
well be slightly different for each person.

> It took 'Butterfly' quite some time to find that door. He came to the
> CATTP when he was five years old. In the beginning he could not
> stay more than five seconds with any one instrument. He had to flutter
> from one instrument to the next, touch everything, knock on every
> instrument and object and activate every switch in the room. In the
> large garden he could not help but keep running after all the butter-
> flies he saw. It seemed as if they were cousins of his that would tell him
> something valuable about his own inner nature. He was always full of

energy and quite difficult to control. He had an unusual ability to see right through people and to bring their weaknesses into the open. This attribute had pushed his mother beyond her limits more than once and had provoked her at times to be too repressive. A vicious circle had formed between mother and child.

Then one day he stayed longer than usual with a clay flowerpot swinging the beater inside the pot from wall to wall, producing the sound of the pot quite delicately. After some three or four minutes, he looked at me calmly and said simply: 'church bell'! All had been said. Finally he had stepped through the gate of sound. After this he would be able to find it whenever he needed to.

When a child moves across a threshold something changes in their eyes; their mental energy field expands, their horizon opens up. Beyond opening themselves up to the essential component in music (-therapy) there is suddenly a sense of space around them. The whole atmosphere seems to relax. One can almost feel a sigh of relief. In entering the experience of sound, consciousness slides from the head to the heart area, from thinking to feeling. This again helps to improve the child's contact with his body and through that with the emotions. This threshold is a necessary condition in order to get into the pleasure of playing music, the pleasure of enjoying music, of playing with sounds and feeling joyful.

'Grasshopper' was able to reproduce any rhythm I showed him, even quite complex ones. It was astonishing to see with what ease, exactness and rapidity a six-year-old could play them. In fact he could copy the rhythms to an extent that would defeat many an adult. His problem was that he could not enjoy them, even though he was perfectly capable of enjoyment when playing outside in the CATTP garden.

He knew instinctively how to repeat a rhythmical cell but could not engage his body and his heart in what he was doing. As a consequence of that he was unable to keep a rhythm. He could find no interest in doing so. Consequently you could not dance to his drumming. Likewise, he would be able to reproduce a series of up to ten notes on the xylophone, rhythmically and melodically correct. However, he could not play them in a continuous flow (water). His music playing happened between his head and his hands. That was all. Therefore he could not be creative musically or 'build' anything musically. When he was playing one thing I could see that his thoughts were already straying somewhere else, a bit like a dog who walks along his path turning his head while his nose is already picking up a new smell.

The metaphor is not too far-fetched since on a psycho-energetic level 'Grasshopper' was actually living most of the time 'up in the air' element. He badly needed to balance his energy by getting a better contact with the water area (fluidity in his rhythms) and with the element of earth (concentration and presence). I kept explaining to him the importance of learning to enjoy himself while he was doing something in the music session. When I asked him to sing and to sway his body from side to side while we played a rhythm together, he would whisper the singing (threshold of the voice) and was not able to get into the body movement that could be compared to the trance-like technique where he could become absorbed by the music, letting the music move his body so as to let go of his obsessive thinking – thus would he slip into experience.

WORKING SUGGESTIONS

Certain emotions and/or the suppression of the feeling of the emotion will keep a person from entering into the experience of sound. To have access to feelings you must first have access to your emotions. I make a distinction here between *emotions* (being a painful experience) and *feelings* (being a non-painful experience). Experiencing sound is about feeling. I have already commented on this: to have access to one's emotions, a person's body contact needs to be improved and the expression of emotion encouraged. Music is a very good means both to express emotions and to improve contact with one's body through, for instance, beating on a large drum with all one's might.

Recently, I had some good results with an autistic boy by creating a constant containing envelope of sound. In this way I provided *earth* and a *mothering* aspect at the same time. I was playing a guitar in open tuning with one hand, beating the drum in a steady rhythm with the other and chanting at the same time. 'Chanting', unlike singing, does not use words or much melody (left side of the brain) but rather emphasises sounds (right side of the brain). The steady rhythm together with the other elements established an ambience providing a *trance-like effect*. For the first time 'Squirrel' started to sing while exploring different instruments at the same time. He seemed finally to let go. The fact that I was busy may have given him the feeling of not being watched, possibly taking away some pressure, while at the same time I was providing this secure background atmosphere.

Quite a number of times I have had to intervene and put an end to a child's stereotypical behaviour and non-musical actions. I did this only when I felt the child was ready in order to give him a chance to get into the experience of sound. I might then say: 'We want music-making here and not noise!' Noise-making can be a first step into sound but it is too often under the power of aggressive emotions.

Getting access to dynamism – fire

The *fire* element is located in the solar plexus area, between navel and sternum. This is where we are most strongly affected by other people's emotions (see solar plexus chakra), causing us to feel invaded and flooded by these emotions. If in certain situations we have experienced an emotional shock without being able to express ourselves adequately – fearing to be punished if we did so, for example – we will most likely be holding onto that experience, having stored it away in our subconscious memory (see etheric) without first 'digesting' it properly. The consequence is that our solar plexus has remained vulnerable and will keep attracting similar experiences so as to learn to deal with them adequately. If again we cannot handle a similar situation we would be holding onto our fear of it happening again. This in turn will inhibit us in the expression of fire ('spitting fire'). Our fire element will be suffocated, held back, and will sooner or later result in timidity, shyness and vulnerability in our meetings with other people. Lack of fire allows us to hold onto fear instead of expressing our love and understanding (the two polarities of the solar plexus) towards ourselves and others. This in turn will reduce the energy in our heart chakra. Instead of generosity, compassion, feelings, inspiration and joy we would rather more easily find ourselves in a depressive state (the two polarities of the 'heart').

Accordingly, it is quite important to check that a patient can properly access his or her emotions and is able to express them. We can work with the theme of fire by encouraging someone to express fire in various forms: imitating a lion's roar, a dragon spitting fire, acting out lightning and mighty thunder on a drum and expressing fire in all its aspects:

explosion, spark, light, warmth, sunshine. Musically-speaking the appropriate characteristic is *dynamic* (loud and soft) and muscular tonus.

'Hobbit' had spent his first few sessions in music therapy crouching near the door, showing me only his left side, so avoiding looking at me or at any musical instrument in the room. Through this posture he showed me that he was not there out of his own free will and did not see how he could participate in the session. Luckily there is a 'hiding corner' in the room with a large beaver shape pillow that happened just to be in front of Hobbit. Soon he decided to hide underneath the beaver. I suggested to him to be a lion sleeping in his cavern with a warning to anyone coming too close and disturbing his sleep. I was aware that Hobbit had a natural sense of humour, being one aspect of his qualities. For several sessions thereafter, he used to hide behind the large frame drum that I placed upright between us for that purpose. Feeling unobserved Hobbit would finally creep out of his cavern, silently approach the drum and give it a mighty beating before hurrying back into his hiding corner. I would leave him just enough time to withdraw before popping up myself from behind the drum and wondering aloud and surprised, who might have been doing this because I could not see anyone. Hobbit laughed – the ice was broken. We have used that game for a number of weeks in music therapy, at times encouraging him to roar like a lion and overcome his great timidity which had been generated by his father's overwhelming outbursts of anger. Hobbit had opened the door to *fire*. The next step in music therapy could begin.

Other children have had to overcome their fear of the sound of the cymbal – an instrument especially affecting the fire area – or of beating loudly on the drum. Often I would encourage them to use their voice while beating strongly on the drum. We would growl and shout aloud while imitating thunder. You must use all your body to beat the drum strongly. Ultimately you have to draw the energy to beat the drum like this from your belly, the hara area. We must not forget that we are brought up in a culture that usually tells children not to be noisy, not to shout or to be rebellious even when the child is being the victim of injustice. Fortunately, we do not always succeed, but the damage is all too often done anyhow. If we suppress fire in our homes and families, the power of fire will be out of control in our societies as evidenced by weapons, explosions, terrorism, nuclear energy and forest fires for example. Everything is linked together.

Getting access to rhythm – water

'Silver' had been quite unable to grasp the phenomenon of rhythm. He could not perceive rhythm as being something different from a simple pulse. I tried just about every thing that came to my mind, but nothing helped. Neither playing the same rhythm on his back, nor singing it, nor playing it on the drum or on any other instrument, nor dancing it in front of him, nor explaining it, nor writing it would help. He remained quite impermeable to the phenomenon and continued to play his pulse, that is a regular and continuous beat without interruption and accent. He loved coming to music and above all he loved playing the drum. He was actually very good at tuning into the speed of any pulse. As soon as I sang a song he would pick up the correct pulse in it and play it. For more than a year though I could not make him understand the difference. I wrote to Norman Weinberger by internet and asked him for advice. He suggested playing two beats and then simply waiting for a while before playing the next two beats. So I did and it worked. Maybe the glimpse of hope on my side was quite an important part in this achievement for if you cannot imagine a solution being possible, you create something in the mental field of the persons present that blocks the process from going any further. Anyhow, that day Silver spontaneously played his first rhythm, and quite a complex one that I had not shown him. In the break afterwards I caught him walking around with a plastic bin under his arm happily beating another rhythm as if it was the most natural thing in the world. He was very pleased with himself, but was probably quite unaware of what had happened.

Many times after this experience I noticed how difficult it can be for children and for some adults to move over this particular threshold.

Further on I will describe what changes in the whole structure of a being might be involved in this process.

Any baby will sometimes create a regular pulse when moving. Normally these rhythmical movements only last a few moments. It is an unconscious movement, instinctive, reflecting some excitement or the taking up of contact with an object. Sometimes this rhythmical contact can have the simultaneous function of creating a sound envelope. The baby will probably be aware of the sound he creates while tapping on the object. While all rhythm is an alternation between 'event' and 'non-event', thus forming the basis of consciousness, tapping a pulse though would remain largely unconscious or subconscious. Usually we do not count the pulses. You just do them and somehow get lost in the activity. Being a pulse is by definition an event that is repeated endlessly, without awareness of time, it may even dissolve time. This is why it is used to induce a state of trance, which in its positive version leads us into beingness, the timeless present. We can find pulse in all music, in all rituals and chants. It is made by North American Indians, by the Saami in Norway, by Siberian shamans, in Africa, anywhere and everywhere. In every case these kinds of rituals try to transcend time. Time does not count anymore.

This pulsating movement is found in the rocking of a baby's cradle, the heart beat, breathing, many rhythms of the brain, and so on. Even when you hammer in a nail you would not choose a waltz rhythm to do so, would you? That is what is meant by pulsation.

Rhythm on the other hand can be counted. It brings us towards dance and asks for a conscious use of our body, that is a better integration of head and body, mental and physical. You need to perceive a rhythm before you can tell the body to dance it. Moving from pulse to rhythm you come out of a fog and become more present, more conscious. The 'I' becomes owner of the body. While rhythm is leading to dance, dance brings joy, what a pulse might just not do. You can forget yourself, forget obsessional thinking in pulse and trance dance for a while. In order to play a rhythm the head alone will not do. You need to live it and integrate it into the memory of your body (see 'etheric' in Chapter 1). In order to move across the threshold of rhythm it is very likely that you will first have to move across the threshold of sound.

I have already described what happens in the brain when working with rhythm and sequential treatment and how it can improve language (see the section at the beginning of this chapter called 'Neuroscience and psycho-energetic approach').

WORKING SUGGESTIONS

I realised how important it was to include the whole body when learning rhythms. Often when teaching rhythms to a child in music therapy I find myself playing a trance-type background, guitar or monochord, drum or rattle and singing underlining the regularity of the pulse and the stability of the sounding envelope. Then at times I would sway my body back and forth or from side to side. Some children copy these movements. This seems to calm them down a lot while their beating on the drum and sometimes their singing become more lively and intense. It is as if the whole being was becoming involved. Doing this, 'Grasshopper' finally let himself glide into enjoying playing music and forgot to think about anything else for a while. It is absolutely necessary to be in one's body in order to concentrate and to be present.

Getting access to creativity – water and space

I remember 'Rabbit', 'Elf' and 'Heron'. All three of them, at different moments, had stepped across the threshold of creativity. Therapeutic work needs to perceive the existence of a threshold and then to use the 'carrot' and the 'stick', pleasure and determination, with the child to allow him to go beyond his limitation. It is not about learning a technique to master an instrument. Much more is at stake and crossing a threshold implies deep changes in the structure of the whole being. Inability to step over a threshold is often brought about by belief structures, thought patterns, habits as well as by neurological patterns. Confronting an absence of creativity for months and months is not a pleasant experience either for the therapist or the patient. This particular threshold is linked to the energy centre of the hara, in the belly area and is most of the time associated with anger and boredom. The child or the adult finds it difficult to endure being confronted with musical instruments that mercilessly keep silent if not played.

If I remember clearly, in all three cases, a day came when I felt that this uncomfortable situation had lasted long enough. I had been working with 'Rabbit', 'Elf' and 'Heron' individually over a period of between one and two years. We had had beautiful moments together, had been joking, had laughed. But music has to be *played*. You cannot avoid that. I felt that the stuck situation had to come to an end and that it was not an extraordinary thing to have fun musically with instruments and to try things out with them. This was particularly so since I did not expect anything special in terms of melodic or rhythmic performance or anything else. To this end I suggested to each one of them that starting in the next session they had to create something in music, a little melody, invent a song or a sound painting using several instruments, or invent anything else musical they liked. I added that I had spent long enough showing them several playing techniques. With Rabbit I had to insist that we were here to play music and not to make noise. With the others I had to repeat that we were not here to use the instruments for non-musical purposes, such as cooking, building shelters and bridges or pieces of artillery. The day came for each of them when I felt I had to talk to them as I would talk to adults.

To my surprise this worked each time. The following week 'Elf' arrived declaring he would now play the song of the moon. This lasted maybe a minute. Then he wanted to play the song of the church of his grandparents' town. In this way he played five or six creations each session, visibly happy about his achievements. Needless to say, each time I was deeply moved to see a child suddenly move out of a long lasting stuck state of being into creative expression and exploration. Another child began by surrounding himself with instruments, turning his back to me while launching into a very long song, not anything quite like Bach or Mozart but certainly just as full of intensity.

Creativity is linked, as I have previously mentioned, to the energy centre of the hara (vitality, sexuality, body contact) and the element of water together with the energy centre of the thyroid (expression) and its element of space. Predictably, when someone starts living their creativity, they experience more fluidity in their whole behaviour and their mental space expands. In the opposite state a person projects an impression of dammed up water, showing excessive rigidity and inflexibility. This can be seen in someone's way of thinking as well as in their body's movements and how they play music. They are just not playful in the way they think or move from one musical idea to another. They are not venturesome. When something does not work, they quickly abandon it.

The source of this rigidity, this feeling of a dam is due to the excessive interference from thoughts, stemming from one or more authorities, such as parents, teachers, uncles and aunts who have imposed their own rigidity on the child who consequently loses his naturalness. When the natural flow of creativity is blocked aggression and frustration are obviously triggered and this may sometimes lead to obsessive behaviour and boredom. The passage from boredom to creativity is in fact a movement away from an external authority into one's own authority. On the level of a society this is a move away from fascism to individuality and creativity. Someone who is really creative is inspired by their own sources, they know their own value or at least are starting to perceive it. Whenever a person displays any authentic natural creativity he starts to show his individuality, to expose himself, sticking his neck out and taking the risk of triggering reactions in others.

This crossing over from creative paralysis to creativity brings relief and joy. It is as if a bird had rediscovered its own natural way of singing. It does not matter how creativity shows itself. Everyone has their own inclinations, their own faculties. The important thing is to let it flow, like water from the source. In this connection I believe that it is quite helpful not to let oneself be influenced and limited by musical habits. Being creative can lead someone to change tonal systems, to use forgotten modes, to tuning an instrument differently for example (Perret 1997).

Having access to one's own creativity does not mean that all the difficulties are completely over. This is especially so with children, but to some extent is the same for adolescents and adults. They need encouragement or at the very least no suppressive interference. For instance, when 'Rabbit' left the CATTP he asked me to get a copy of the video I had filmed of some of his sessions. Seven months later I started to do additional work in another part of the hospital, a day clinic for children between eight and thirteen. There I met 'Rabbit' again and carried on working with him. He reminded me to get him a copy of the video. I finally gave him one, but now I regret it. I suspect that his jealous elder brother and possibly his parents too, did not realise what an achievement his creative singing had been for him. Perhaps he got some devaluing remarks about his work shown on the video, because in music therapy he was blocked again for several weeks after I had given him the copy. Luckily his creative urge was stronger and he overcame that phase.

Memory of a creative phase may last for a period of time. The 'flame', though, needs oxygen. Individual creativity and vitality never die, but they can be stored away in the subconscious where they may possibly remain out of sight and inaccessible. We need to bear in mind that creativity is not about creating 'art' or commercial items. The value of creativity, individually as much as socially, is independent of external approval or commercial values. A lot of so called artwork is given far too much importance and is distorted in value by market mechanisms. It puts a few on a pedestal and pays them richly for acting out what actually everyone should be and can be doing. That is another story.

I remember the self-validating experience music sessions had for a male prisoner in a prison where I worked for four years. He had had several bad clashes with prison wardens because of his significant authority conflict and dammed up anger. A prison is a very difficult place to deal with this. In reality there was no way he could be right when disagreeing with a prison warden. In the case of an injustice he had hardly any rights at all which would allow him to correct the situation. He ended up by turning his violent emotions against himself, cutting his lower arms with razor blades or anything he could find. He did not know how to play any musical instrument but said he would love to try the drum kit. He was obviously gifted for playing it. The fact of having a role to play in a group, of having a highlight in his weekly prison routine, and of being able to talk with other people as equal to equal, as well as being able to express himself on a drum kit brought joy back into his life and allowed him to forget his destructiveness for a while.

The passage from destructiveness to creativity needs a minimum of support. I remember two men from Tunisia who attended the music sessions in the prison. It was obvious that they knew how to play music but they could only join in the creative process on the day when I encouraged them to play their own traditional music. They started with a piece of 'Rai' and then, feeling accepted by the group, in a very short time found a great joy in playing music. As this prison had inmates from a large number of different countries, we had the great pleasure of having phases of playing music from Angola, a beguine from Guadeloupe alternating with rock-and-roll and pop songs. There were many unforgettable moments.

How can we detect through musical playing, when someone is being creative? If the sessions last over a period of time this can be easier. It is not difficult, though, to recognise when someone is not building anything up in a music session, when he is not enjoying any of the instruments he is trying out or when he or she is just repeating quite stereotypical patterns. Getting pleasure from the experience of sound can be detected. It is necessary but not enough. To get into a creative exploration is an additional step, that is when the whole person seems to light up. This may last only a brief moment but we can feel that she is expressing something that matters to her. The important thing is not a melody, a composition or suchlike; a succession of notes or beats revealing a meaning, some sort of intensity and some joy are sufficient. The difference may seem subtle but will be of great consequence.

Accessing the spontaneous use of voice – space

In my courses I give a lot of time to solo improvisation. I encourage the person to let go of any preconceived idea, she should not simply reproduce things that she may already know so as to get approval from the audience. A very particular pleasure is to hear someone improvise with his voice. In doing this one is in a certain way standing there naked. It may feel difficult to start but there is nothing like the voice for adapting quickly to a new idea, a sudden change. The voice offers the improviser a very wide range of possibilities. Every time someone sings spontaneously, it is always as if it were for the first time. It is simple and at the same time enriching for everyone present.

Singing, of course, is linked to the thyroid chakra. The voice is a true mirror, rich and complete, of our whole psycho-energetic state. It has the advantage of showing quite unmistakably how we feel (Perret 1997).

When an adult launches into a spontaneous improvisation with the voice it may happen that we express something completely unexpected. The voice not only reflects our emotions, it can reveal sound spaces sometimes very unfamiliar to us, sometimes even from past lives, sounds the origins of which are completely unknown to us but which open rich and unexpected spaces. When this happens all the people present experience an unforgettable moment. The depth, the incredible strength that may come forth and the quality of truth that such an event can transmit may even 'rock the boat' of our mundane lives. More than once the person singing has stepped out from that experience transformed.

A spontaneous expression with his voice is an important threshold for a child to cross and it remains open as a doorway always able to show us the way into new spaces if we wish to enter them.

Getting access to the melodic organisation – air

Grasping the melodic organisation of an instrument requires a sense of the musical system used on it. This opens up the possibility to create tunes or musical patterns with sense. This may seem easy to an adult but it is certainly not so for the children who come to the day clinic. The brain will do this job only when it is ready for it, for while the experience of sound is mainly located in the brain's right hemisphere, an understanding of the melodic organisation seems to be located in the left hemisphere. It is similar to grasping the difference between the shape of a letter and its logical significance. So it is likely that a child will cross this threshold around the same time that he is learning the structure of the alphabet which opens up the way for him to read and understand what he reads.

Again the first step seems to be linked to the child's interest in exploring the value of different musical notes, experiencing their sound and comparing them. A second step must be taken for the child to realise consciously that the low notes are at one end and the high notes at the other. Understanding then that the notes are set out in a systematic order is yet another step. This is what we label the 'melodic organisation' of an instrument. Memory plays a part here, since one has to memorise how the notes sound and where we heard each different sound. The child has to reproduce the order in her brain or rather in her memory. We do not actually know whether or not memory happens in the brain itself. The memorising process can be seen to be activating neurones in the brain, but the memory itself may be stored elsewhere. I suggest that this happens in the etheric energy field. It is only after taking this step that a child will understand the melodic organisation of the instrument and can start to construct his playing more consciously. This in turn will be more meaningful and more satisfying. However, I am still not talking here about reading music, even if the two processes may be linked.

Playing a melody, even a short one, almost certainly uses both hemispheres of the brain for the simple reason that this activity usually relates more to feeling than to just reading words. Working with children so that they grasp the melodic organisation of an instrument may be a way to help children who have difficulties learning to read, precisely because the right side of the brain is engaged in the musical task.

WORKING SUGGESTIONS

I proceed in different ways. Sometimes I play short sequences of notes on the xylophone so that the child or the adult can repeat them. There may be a rhythmical structure in it or not. This approach is classical. I may also play a sequence of notes belonging to a well known melody. If the child is already showing interest in the alphabet, I may play a sequence and point out the 'name' of the note written on the actual note on the xylophone: 'A', 'G', 'E' and so on. 'Grasshopper' was able to repeat any complex sequence of rhythmically played notes without having the slightest idea of the organisation of the notes on the instrument. He needed first to go through the experience of sound, to let the instrument 'sink in'. I have mentioned him before. Do not forget that a child may often store up what he has learned for a period of time before demonstrating his newly learned ability to someone else. After a delay of three or four weeks the apparently forgotten sequence may pop up in a session.

Permanent goals in (musical) expression

Practising harmony – like human growth – never reaches its goal. Everything is just preparation for a further step. While these permanent goals are present from the very first session, their guiding value never lessens.

Ability to harmonise and balance

All five elements need to be present to a greater or lesser degree in any balanced expression. When one wants to improve a person's musicality this is the first thing to check. Only when the five elements are present will the person's expression possibly start to radiate and be able to move the listener.

Ability to move someone and be radiant

Of what is this quality made? How do we acquire it? What can we suggest to a person who wants to improve his musicality, beyond watching out for any imbalances between the five elements (Perret 1997)?

Expressing joy

Joy and intensity are my first two criteria when working with someone musically. Joy brings a lightness of heart, one might call it a spiritual dimension, that transports us way beyond our emotions and daily worries. Music is a great means for spreading joy.

Creating intensity

Intensity is a mystery. It obviously manifests itself when the whole being is engaged, one might say that the soul is visibly coming through. Certainly intensity does not belong in the category of painful emotions. The person displays a certain curiosity, a special concentration, a phenomenon on an energy level as if an inner string was starting to vibrate. It is difficult to describe. Nevertheless intensity seems to be the signal that something fundamental is happening, is getting established and that thereafter anything might happen. It is as if magic starts to operate. We seem to be propelled into the core of things, time is suspended for a while. Even if no immediate result is detectable, I know we are on the right track and that it will not be long before results will show in one form or another. When there is intensity present I am convinced that an inner intelligence is taking over and guiding us on the way to healing, as if the soul had taken the steering wheel.

'Whirlwind' was an autistic child. In music therapy it was quite obvious that he was in another state of mind. He would keep himelf busy with exploring music instruments throughout any session. I felt that his choice of an instrument was guided from inside. I felt this when for weeks he used to walk around holding the rainstick to his ear in order to feel better the sound of falling 'rain'. Very likely when intensity is visible there is a balance in the use of the two hemispheres of the brain.

Sometimes it does not take much for intensity to take over. For some two years I gave a weekly music atelier in a sheltered workshop for adults with special needs. A tall lady about forty years old was always there but she remained in the background for months. I felt that she would have liked to play but was too shy. One day I gave her a small hand drum and asked her to play in her own way. She took the drum, playing it very tentatively at first. After a few minutes, seeing that she still had all our attention, she accelerated her beat slightly. Some two minutes later maybe, she speeded up again finally getting into an extraordinary intensity…and she had a big smile on her face that I will never forget. Unfortunately the workshop was stopped a short time after that. The parents and the majority in the team of carers could not see any point in playing music with these people and had not understood what it could mean for them and bring to them. Prejudice about people with special needs had taken over again. It showed me once more that the mentally disabled are not always those people we think to label 'disabled'.

Taking part in creative musical communication

Creative musical communication takes place between two or more people present. It is a meeting on a feeling level. We can watch this happening of course in jazz, but it is also present in our improvisations when we create soundscapes together, whether with children or adults, disabled or not. In fact with soundscapes or 'musical paintings' anyone can join in, everyone is equal. The choice of the instruments is crucial of course. If simple-to-play instruments such as xylophones, percussion, drums are offered (see the list in Appendix 1) there will not be any technical difficulties to master.

Surrendering to inspirational expression

The ultimate goal is not to obstruct oneself and to allow oneself to be carried away by an inspirational current when this occurs. We know rather little about where our musical impulses come from when they cannot be simply traced back to things we have heard before. We can speculate though. Once we can establish a balance between feeling and expression, between our inner reality and our music, anything can happen. We can anticipate anything and may in particular expect surprises. I have witnessed people expressing features which evidently have come forward from past lives, from distant cultures, distant in time or space. I have seen other improvisations clearly coming forth from a place of inner wisdom, some bearing a vision for the future, some coming from a deep love for nature and the elements. I have witnessed many other improvised expressions beyond the reach of words. Each time an incredible intensity was present, a sense of truth and wisdom. These moments were very uplifting, bringing unexpected treasures and insights.

Silence, receptivity, space and listening

You can read about the importance and ramifications of the element space in the chapter on the five elements.

Parallel changes in the general behaviour of the person

The significance of a neuro-musical threshold must reveal itself through positive changes in someone's behaviour. I discovered the existence of these thresholds because I could observe:

- the absence of a certain quality in a person's musical expression

- a noticeable and prolonged resistance to remedying that absence by crossing over a certain threshold

- significant and lasting changes in behaviour once the threshold was crossed

- concordant observations by my colleagues, by parents, teachers and other professionals working outside the CATTP.

I have searched through different sets of criteria for evaluating behaviour hoping to find reliable facts that can be observed and which would underline the importance of these thresholds. At first detailed rating schemes dealing with the developmental steps of young autistic children seemed to encourage my search (see Appendix 4 on the rating scheme by Haag).

I have not, however, been successful up to now in finding similar and satisfying criteria that could be applied to non-autistic children or which could be relevant for adolescents and adults. Because I am working mainly with children suffering from pervasive developmental disorder, who do not necessarily belong in the autistic spectrum, the rating schemes mentioned above are insufficient as far as the observation of neuro-musical thresholds is concerned. One can find a multitude of rating scales relevant to young children up to the age of three. In music therapy I am working mostly with children above the age of three. Cognitivists have created very detailed rating scales concerning perception, fine motor capacities, eye–hand co-ordination and cognitive performance. However those schemes present very little about emotions, the imaginary dimension, social capacities or a person's qualities (Schopler *et al.* 1994).

The most satisfying *evaluation procedure* I have come across in literature is Amelia Oldfield's as she describes it in T. Wigram: *Assessment and evaluation in the arts therapies*. She structures her session in such a way that she knows how each section lends itself to observe a certain selection of criteria. No rating scale but rather the awareness comparable to a psychotherapist who would observe in a thorough way and knows what she is looking for. My evaluation sheet (Appendix 6) is just another trial in that direction.

In evaluation meetings it happened more than once that most team members would have kept their noses glued to the heaviness of a child's situation and how little progress was made, how little prospect there was for him, etc., had we not been able to glimpse the dormant, yet perceivable qualities of that child that were there. It is this level of contact that can help in trusting and finding the appropriate therapeutic goals for the patient.

Ultimately in my approach I would want to stay aware of furthering soul expression, including expression of the individual's qualities, compassion, contentment, calmness, joy, awareness, trust, faith, acceptance of present situation (including oneself), before any musial achievement (musical skills, expression, communication), or even degrees of active participation.

Some levels of work will clearly belong to therapy (aiming primarily at improvement of social behaviour, language, emotional stability, independence, etc. and being within the limits, for example of what a public health system can take care of), while the other levels would be part of personal development and spiritual healing.

I am very aware that more research is needed to standardise my observations and to make them more easily recognisable and useful. It is my dearest wish. For the moment though I have got to describe them with my own means. In my view, observation using the five elements and neuro-musical thresholds is viable and sufficiently detailed. This approach is not widespread of course and demands some experience before it can be applied.

Moreover, it is very likely that the way I work with the children at the CATTP, and more generally with adults and students, does not lend itself easily to standardised observations where you need only to tick the appropriate box in order to catch the essential aspects of a change. A patient can very well make significant progress about his self-esteem, the contact with his qualities, with spiritual values, without this being immediately translated onto a cognitive or physical level.

I shall try to explain this with the help of a metaphor. Let us consider a child who is learning how to ride a bicycle. It may take him several weeks to find the right speed and balance that will allow him to ride on two wheels without falling. This will require the co-ordination of an impressive number of processes. The balance needed is very specific, but his efforts to acquire that specific balance will at the same time be very revealing about a number of other inner processes and abilities. Neuro-musical thresholds seem to be comparable. Each one of them may be the witness to a global improvement of performance on an emotional, physical and mental level. As to the permanent goals, they bear witness to an integration of higher levels of consciousness, such as the influx of spiritual energy into the heart chakra thus leading to less depression or into the thyroid chakra thus leading to a better expression of one's emotions and needs.

Let us take another example: to speak with coherent phrases of five words, a considerable number of processes must be operating in the brain. These processes in turn depend on a number of other functions, for instance a desire to understand what other people say, to be understood by them and to communicate with them. Communication is of course much more than packing information into a slightly melodic sequence of words. Scientists have been working on these questions so as to understand the various pathologies of language and how to heal them.

What do we know, however, of the mechanisms leading to joy, expansion, trust in oneself, serenity or a warm-hearted expression? Can they all be found in the brain? Changes can always be observed in concrete action, but maybe what is visible is only the tip of the iceberg. Changes may be far more important than what is suggested by the effects that can be observed from the outside. This being said, all team members at the CATTP, parents and teachers, generally agree when a child demonstrates major changes even if they cannot always accurately describe the changes with words. Deep changes happen on an energy level, I believe.

I love working with people with disabilities. So often they do have a very good heart. Many have speaking difficulties as well as mental and physical difficulties. This leads to situations where they often feel that they are not understood and are not being seen as human beings with feelings and with real needs to grow. For such people changes in behaviour often show up in less frustration, more joy, being calmer and more serene and in an overall feeling of living a more satisfying life. Which rating scale would take into consideration that someone disabled has a good heart, feels happier, is more confident, is more aware of their own inner value? I believe it is very important to be conscious of those deeper changes.

To observe a shift from the emotional level towards a higher level of consciousness using the help of the five elements, observations using both right and left brain hemispheres is essential. Here are some examples of detectable changes in behaviour that follow the structure of the five elements (see also Appendix 6, the evaluation sheet using the five elements).

When the element of earth is in a process of transformation, positive changes in the person's sense of *security*, in the individual's capacity to *concentrate* and *trust* will develop. Probably there would also be an improved contact with the ground, the feet and legs. This should be observable in how the person walks and sets their feet on the ground. An improvement concerning the earth level can show in a child's diminished need to cling to the adult as he is now able to find his own security in himself. There will be similar signs for people who always needed to be the centre of attention, for children who cannot play on their own. People who are too '*speedy*' and are stuck in their heads would start to be calmer and less frenetic. Their speediness might of course also include an underlying fear (fire) and a blockage in the diaphragm.

Destructive tendencies (water) usually have two aspects. *Aggression* towards others can be selective and may be directed especially towards women or children, for example. *Self-destructive* tendencies, although generated in the water element, can also manifest in the air element by depressive withdrawals. As the thyroid chakra is itself reflecting what is happening in the lower four chakras, it will always be affected by changes. Accordingly, the patient's expression would change, including her speech, body movement, ways of thinking, expression of emotions and feelings. Another form of destructive behaviour is the urge *not to respect the structure* and rules of the therapy session. Concerning the water element there can of course be a change in the cleanliness of the child (being able to go to the toilet when necessary, for example). Improvement in the water element would, as we have seen before, mean a better vitality, a better flow of creative ideas, improved contact with the body, less violent, brisk and harsh movements.

Phobias, fears and *anxieties* are all signs of a lack of fire and are all linked to the functioning of the solar plexus chakra. Improving and healing the fire element often requires simultaneous working with the earth and the water element. The person will eventually be showing more warmth in their being and a clear decline in an obsessive tendency to want to control everything and everyone.

A major change in behaviour happens when a person becomes able to express emotions and can state his or her limits better or express anger when appropriate (water and fire). It is of course easy to see when a person becomes able to express joy, show feelings and tenderness. An improvement in the air element would bring about lightness, joy and a sense of beauty, being able to notice beauty around oneself.

There are a list of obvious signs to watch out for such as the improvement of digestion, sleep, skin diseases, allergies and all the signs which would belong to the judgement of a medical doctor. It is probably most appropriate to draw one's own evaluation criteria according to the age group, pathologies, etc. A standardisation of criteria may after all not prove very useful in practice. The sharp collective 'eye' of a team, the therapist's work with supervision so as to avoid dead ends and a free-flowing communication between the professionals in charge of the therapeutic work are more important things on which to focus. This may include an awareness of the balance of the five elements within the institution itself, or within oneself in the case of a single therapist. The presence of spiritual values such as beauty, calmness, harmony, peace, understanding, compassion, love, meaning, joy, patience, creativity are at the top of the list and not just for the patient's expression.

Snake Dance (excerpt)

At the corner of my eye I notice the grass moving, as I look I realise it's moving a lot, maybe a mouse or a mole about to surface, when suddenly two heads appear above the grass. Snakes, grass snakes, not far from me. They see me and freeze. We are invisible, we are not alive, we are grass. I catch my breath and freeze too, and silently tell them I will do you no harm, no harm, you are safe. What will they do? I don't move, nor do they, who will break this spell? They almost look comical, two heads motionless above the grass, my body on full alert, tingling all over, holding my breath. They are long, about one meter or more, snakes, grass snakes, no harm. We three stay frozen only for a couple of minutes, yet it seems like time stops. I am also still aware of the swallows looping, the crickets in the grass, bees buzzing past, all the intense life movement that keeps on flowing as we three wait.

Suddenly they are moving and I can breathe again. They are quivering even higher now, bodies entwined, one twists and spirals all around the other's body. Starting at the neck, the throbbing, pulsating rhythm goes down to the tails. Now still, bound together in each other's no arms no legs embrace, amongst the flowers, catching their breaths. Then off again, heads rising high above the grass, cruising smoothly through the green meadow. Then again a wild and passionate coupling, a pulsating spiral from neck to tail. Then up and up again, cruising together, throbbing spiralling, rhythmic, bursting snake dance. The intense heat of 'cold blooded' snake love.

Marie Perret, 2004

Chapter 4

Teacher, Musician, Therapist or Shaman?

Therapy and development: two approaches – one axis

I have tried throughout the book to underline the common points in the work of a musician, a music teacher and a music therapist. All musical activity involves harmony and harmonising. In its nature it is basically therapeutic or healing. Let us look at this more closely.

We can define as *therapeutic* all work that aims to help a person overcome a pathology, an illness or a strong crisis, whereas *pedagogical* work is concerned to help a person who is in 'good health' (mentally and physically) to develop her skills further. We can designate as *personal development* all work on oneself designed to develop one's spiritual potential or one's innate qualities. I feel strongly that all these activities should be placed along the same line whose middle point would mark a hypothetical state called 'well-being'. On the therapeutic side of this point we would be moving towards that state of well-being, on the other side of the point we would want to develop ourselves further through personal evolution and educational work. On each side of the middle point work and activities are pursued with the aim of helping someone evolve, of guiding him towards a fuller unfolding of his potential, of inborn qualities. The person receives what she is ready for and the teacher or therapist transmits what he knows and has already integrated for himself. The ways of working on both sides of that imaginary middle point are not fundamentally different. Howard Gardner, in his theory of artistic development (1994) emphasises that musical development has got to be holistic, that is, it must be an integrative process.

In my own experience therapeutic action often takes place without a detailed plan for a particular session, without my knowing for sure in advance the effectiveness of what I propose to do. I am aware of the person opposite me and in a larger sense of the energy ambience, the feeling in the room. I watch out for any signs of joy and/or intensity. If I can detect them I know we should continue on the path we are on. If on the contrary dispersion, boredom, resistance prevail, it is very likely we have not yet found the best way to run the session. In that situation I must continue to look for the crack in the defence system, for the least opening of the closed door. Quite often I use humour to keep the working atmosphere light and playful. In all pedagogical and therapeutic activities, as well as in development work we often find ourselves face to face with the unknown. Since we often have real difficulties knowing who we ourselves really are, how should we be able to fully know someone else?

In my work with adults or children at the children's day clinic I could not say at any particular moment which role I am actually playing. Am I more of the therapist, the pedagogue, the musician or at times even the 'shaman'? Who actually knows for sure? Much depends on what the client needs and asks for – explicitly or otherwise – and on how we define these words. When I am clearly working on a person's pathological obstacle, that is on a behaviour trait that stands out from ordinary, 'healthy' behaviour, then I can consider myself to be doing therapeutic work. When I teach a musical technique or suggest a particular change in behaviour, I suppose I am more on the pedagogical side.

I am much in favour of an awareness by the musician and by any person teaching music, that allows him to perceive the healing action involved in musical activities and so never to forget that music connects each of us strongly to our heart and through this to our deepest needs. It is self-evident though, that in order to help someone go beyond his psychological limits, one needs to know what one is doing. A solid training in some form of psychotherapy plus extensive personal experience are absolutely necessary. This cannot be acquired through reading or listening to a teacher, nor is it enough to do personal emotional work in a group. Above all it is necessary to know oneself and through this to know one's own limitations. When a client consciously seeks personal evolution, therapeutic work will lead the client towards finding a new inner balance on a higher level to where he previously was. This implies that such a person will have to leave behind certain thought and belief structures, that until then had provided him with a sense of security, even though only an illusory one. Somehow through the therapeutic encounter the carpet is pulled from underneath his feet (earth), helping him to move towards new horizons (space). This is precisely what Tibetan tradition teaches us when it says, that ultimate security can only be found in the element space, because all other forms of security, being ultimately illusory, will let us down sooner or later.

To return to the question I formulated in the heading of this chapter, who are we really when we work with music to help another person in some way? Are we pedagogues, musicians, therapists or *shamans*? A shaman will essentially have developed right side of the brain techniques, at times using specific and deliberately chosen musical instruments, such as the frame drum or rattles, as well as his/her voice in order to access and to influence a level of consciousness where the deeper cause of an illness can be found. I am convinced that one can find a personal way to work in this field, going beyond the limitations taught by western societies for several centuries. From these millenary shamanic traditions we can learn respect and love for nature and how to live in harmony with the natural elements.

I know only a very little about shamanic traditions in Asia, Africa, Northern Europe, Australia and America. These traditions can be found in all continents among people who have kept a close and respectful link to nature. I am convinced that we of the so-called civilised world will never become exactly like them because we have not been brought up in a shamanic tradition. To think that we can just copy their actions is an illusion and a sign of disrespect for those who maintain these traditions. However, I am convinced that we in western Europe, as well as people everywhere else, once had comparable traditions which embraced the same wisdom, the same deep understanding of nature, of *our* own nature. We still can detect some traces in the Celtic Druidic tradition. There certainly is a strong living tradition in Siberia and amongst the Saami people in Finland and Northern Norway.

I know from the experiences we may have through working with the five elements and their associated animals that we do penetrate into similar levels of consciousness. I am talking here of the natural link between nature and human beings and of the intuitive dimension and knowledge which accumulates from experience in a people that lives in harmony with natural existence. This wisdom is connected to the heart and is expressed as compassion. It is not the result of emotional manipulation in the solar plexus and astral levels. This can happen sometimes but is certainly not the essence nor the exclusivity of shamanism. Fundamentally this wisdom is about respecting an individual's freedom of choice. Here too we need to learn to discriminate, as the French say: 'It is not the dress that makes a monk' and I may add 'nor the feather that makes a shaman'.

Musical transmission as I have described it cannot be limited to learning an artistic discipline and acquiring some playing techniques. The essential elements of musicality are transmitted orally. Some recent research documenting this asserts that: all oral transmission, throughout the ages, has always been more complete and exact than written transmission, no matter how sophisticated. The researchers compared a specific tradition written down at the beginning of the twentieth century with the same tradition orally transmitted. At the end of the century the oral tradition was still active and could therefore be compared with the written form. Jean During has written a wonderful book on the significance of oral tradition in oriental music. He chose a title which has a double meaning in French: 'Quelque chose se passe' (During 1994). This can be translated as 'Something is being passed on' and also as 'Something is happening'. Musical teaching in the oral transmission is essentially a way of learning the mysteries of harmony, in the larger sense of the word. Again, we are not far from shamanism.

Three levels of teaching: shamanic, tantric and essence

Work done with the five elements can take place on three levels which cannot always be separated. There is an external level, an inner level and one labelled the 'pure mind' or essence level (T.W. Rinpoche 2002). The more we can learn to work on a subtle or pure mind level, the better we shall be able to get in touch with the deeper causes of an illness or imbalance.

The *external level* refers to the elements as we find them in nature. It also includes phenomena usually invisible to the naked eye and not detectable by us through the usual five senses. They are energy phenomena connected to certain places and elements, sometimes called 'nature spirits'. Anthroposophy, amongst other traditions, explores this dimension. This level reveals itself to us as soon as we are interested in the ambience of a place, the beauty of a flower, the magic of a tree or a little brook. I mention it in several places in this book as a dimension that reveals itself quite naturally when one works with the five elements. This is also called the *shamanic level*.

In my work on musical expression I often start with an almost panto-mimic level. This might be imitating an actual acoustic manifestation such as the galloping of a horse, the sound of thunder, a mouse's tiny steps on a drum skin, the gurgling of a small brook, the noise generated by a rainstick. In the early stages of their work people often get stuck at that pantomimic level and because of it they rely too much on their thinking. This is why I progressively move towards using feelings and imagination to enter into the quality of the element, leaving behind the acoustic imitation. In this way someone can express any element, earth, water or fire or any feeling and emotion, *anger* or *serenity* for example, using only one instrument such as a drum.

On the *inner level* we are dealing with energy, the elements and their corresponding processes inside our body, rather than physical forms, the human body, plants or animals. Here we find the circulation of our blood and lymph, breathing and the electro-chemical impulses that run along our nerves, our digestive processes and all that is happening in the brain. We can learn to direct our attention to follow our breathing, for instance to improve belly breathing or to enhance the blood circulation through our feet. We are then really working with the energy circulations that we can direct in our body through the energy channels. These are named psychic streams by Bob Moore, nadis in India and acupuncture meridians in China. Sounds combined with awareness can reinforce this process. The psycho-energetic exercises I teach in courses help this kind of work (Perret 1997). The Tibetans call this level of working *tantric*.

Finally there is the level of *pure mind* and here we are dealing with the most subtle level. At this level we are getting in touch with the essence of an element. We are then beyond any duality found in physical appear-ances, emotions or thought concepts. This work happens through medi-tation. It is on this level that the dzogchen teachings operate in the Tibetan tradition. Different names have been given to this kind of work depending on the cultural context. We may also find ourselves going beyond sound into silence into the true nature of mind, emptiness. If sound can help us approach this point, the final steps along the path have to be taken in silence.

Improvisation: some basic rules

Practising harmony while playing music can be done through score reading, through familiarity with oral tradition, in traditional music, rock, rap, reggae and blues for example. Really free improvisation, however, is the best means to join feeling with expression. Free improvisation uses little intellect and does not pay attention to the expectations of either conductor, composer or audience. It encourages free expression of the momentary inner state of the one who is playing.

When I talk about free improvisation in this context, it might be a sound painting or soundscape that does not follow any particular style of music. It is not like a jazz improvisation, not even like a free jazz improvisation since most jazz relies very much on rules and structures. Nor is it any other known type of improvisation such as one finds in Indian ragas or blues music (Perret 1997). Neither is one trying to impress an audience by playing certain musical phrases, using a particular technique or virtuoso fast playing for example, things that have proven admirable and successful in the past. No knowledge, no technical level of skill, no pre-conceived idea, as far as that is possible, should obstruct the free *flow* (water) of inner inspiration.

Depending on the musician's state, I would probably insist on her playing for at least five to fifteen minutes. There may be exceptions of course. Usually, though, it is about this length of time that is necessary for the player to get over her initial inhibitions, to find an opening to deeper levels and to let herself be carried away so that the musical expression will truly reflect what is happening inside. The inner level is not limited to our emotions but may engage any aspect within us which is more or less conscious, for instance the collective unconscious, energy phenomena and spirituality.

It is useful to apply some basic rules which facilitate free improvisation:

1. Having a sufficient mastery of the instrument chosen in order to be able to express oneself unhindered.

2. Knowing how to centre oneself (see Appendix 3 for a centring exercise).

3. Being aware of a direction to take, a felt intention to be followed while playing.

4. Becoming aware of one's degree of concentration.

5. Entering the experience of sound.

6. Accessing a playful way in order to enjoy oneself.

7. Accepting a natural, true and authentic creativity.

8. Allowing oneself to explore and express some craziness if necessary (fire).

9. Remembering that several levels can open up, such a those leading into the qualities of one or more of the five elements and beyond.

10. Bearing in mind that some balance of the five elements is often necessary in order to maintain a creative flow. The characteristics are:

   Earth: not losing contact with a base to which one can return from time to time
   Water: keeping a flow from one element or idea to the next
   Fire: the cathartic, transforming quality, also warmth and love
   Air: softness of feelings, lightness, flying
   Space: giving oneself space during improvisation, silence, non action.

11. Avoiding any analysis during improvisation.

12. Remembering to stop at the right moment.

13. Feeling the need to re-centre oneself briefly at the end.

Any true improvisation of that nature cannot but leave its mark on the player and listener, it transforms them both. Even though as a musician one may never feel entirely satisfied because although aware of a natural flow, some may say from a Divine Source, the player will always remain somewhat of an obstacle, an imperfect instrument. That is acceptable though, and is a part of the game to be played. As well as feelings of joy we may also feel brief moments of vulnerability and possibly even of sadness. The process described here that helps one to access a free improvisation is in fact a means to contact other levels of consciousness. The steps in the process help the player to avoid being controlled by his ego.

When the player is carried away during an improvisation he may not always remain completely aware of all that happens. The musician feels and expresses, but reflection may take place later. It is worth pointing out that this way of improvising can only be used with a mentally well-balanced person, who does not have a personality that is unhealthily underdeveloped, such as someone suffering from schizophrenia.

Feeling

Trying to play what we feel is sometimes more easily said than done. Some people unfortunately seem to have lost all sense of their own feelings. They do not have a usable language of any kind to express their feelings. This language was silenced when they were children. Spontaneous expression such as musical expression, can often bring it back after a few sessions. What is being looked for is nothing more than some musical notes or beats full of intensity. These can reveal all that is necessary to start a therapeutic dialogue. Feelings are practically the only means to gain access to the perception of energy. When we think about that for a while we realise that because feelings are a part of the upper astral they are only accessible when the grosser layer of painful emotions found in the lower astral closer to the physical body are contacted and gradually transformed into feelings.

Consciousness, listening and guidance

Listening with the right hemisphere of the brain – our feeling side – allows us to reach the *roots of musicality* in the person playing before us. We find ourselves tuning in to his psycho-energetic structure, to his energy. However, we can only remain receptive on that level as long as we consciously avoid analysing simultaneously what we perceive. Analysing must come afterwards and is an activity in the left hemisphere of the brain. We may have all kinds of perceptions coming from different levels. The list of levels of perception given in Appendix 5 is not of course exhaustive. There are levels of consciousness which cannot be expressed in words. There is no other way to know of their existence other than first to experience them ourselves. This should not be a reason for anxiety except perhaps for our intellect and personality that may not like this idea. This cannot be helped though, consciousness and the world we inhabit is apparently made like this.

The process of listening and analysing demands experience and above all a good understanding of oneself. This becomes all the more important when we get involved in a therapeutic relationship where what we express is meant to help the other person present to evolve in some way. We must have a sense of what the other person is ready to hear and to assimilate. A person with a very weak sense of self for instance, is not in any state to hear everything one may recognise about him and hear in her playing. To do this would risk the player becoming submerged, water and subconscious, by a tidal wave of emotions that might be disastrous for them and provoke even further disintegration of their personality. On the other hand, a person who has had the opportunity to strengthen his ego in a natural way, who has a sense of his own identity, may very well be ready to open up to new horizons where the every day personality may have a lesser role to play.

Sensitive listening assisted by the five elements system can serve as a powerful mirror for the player. The more one is willing to express oneself truthfully and sincerely, the more material will appear from previously unconscious levels. The process of spontaneous and true expression makes us feel vulnerable and naked at times. It is essential to be gentle and careful with our comments and whenever necessary to protect the player from the projections of other people present in the room. Sometimes having the player watch a video of his performance with little or no comment can be just as much as he may be able to integrate at the time.

A feeling observation may start by detecting the presence or absence of intensity. The more intensity we can feel to be present, the more information may come forth. In either case we can go deeper into our observation with the help of the five elements. Is there a predominance of one element or is the absence of an element detectable? What feelings or overall picture does the listener get? Are there any animals in it, what is the landscape around it, are there other beings, what are the light conditions? Are there specific body zones or places in the energy fields around the player's body that attracts our attention? What does the person think of his own performance? Does he feel that he was able to express authentically what he felt?

Often the observer does not need to say much. The player will know pretty well the quality of what he has played. Helping him to make some connections may be all that is required for him to go further. Very often we find it very difficult to see and accept our good sides, our qualities and strong points. In my approach I suggest that it is imperative to underline these points. Once we restore better contact with our qualities we shall give less and less energy to our old habit of wanting to hide our strengths. These habits may well start melting like snow in the sushine without us having to do anything forceful.

Concerning psychic phenomena, minor clairvoyance or clairaudience, I believe that it is not necessary to give them extra attention. Such phenomena can prove to be strong traps because people may misuse them so as to impress others. Human growth cannot stop on that intermediary level. True growth is not stepping out of one cage just to step into another one.

When a person is ready to let himself go into a therapeutic process I may ask him to improvise freely and spontaneously whatever he feels. I suggest that he launches himself fully into it and avoids as much as possible trying to impress others or hiding behind preconceived ideas and ways of playing. Often it can help to avoid your favourite instrument for a while, the one you are most used to and to play on an instrument that does not have the same musical system. Flowerpots, an untuned percussion or an African balafon can prove very useful. It can help to exchange the keys of a xylophone or metallophone and put them in a different order so that the intellect becomes confused which helps our feelings to take over.

We can also use a feeling perception when music is played from a musical score or by heart. We would just need to differentiate the various filters that would tend to hide the spontaneous aspect, the player's inner world. In order to improve the quality, the radiation of the performance, we may want to work beforehand solely with the five elements and come back to playing from the score later on. Some indications referring directly to the five elements, however, may very well be heard when the player is performing from a music sheet or by heart.

Lucid trance

From a very young age 'Rabbit' had been a prisoner of his seemingly immutable anger. Anything could become a source of his bad humour. He seemed to be particularly reproachful towards the women amongst the staff of the day clinic who represented his own inner female aspect. I had him in music therapy from the age of five to eight. While he always liked coming to music therapy, he soon began to feel bored in the sessions. Early on in the therapy he used to spend quite a bit of time on the drum, playing with a grimace on his face and with very tense movements of the arm, wrist and hand. He could not stop talking obsessively of sewers and pots of all kinds.

He was one of those children who took years to cross the threshold of creativity. But on the day that he crossed this threshold he forgot all about his anger from that day onwards. On the same day he had also crossed the thresholds of spontaneous singing and rhythm. Parallel with this he found himself a ritual of self-healing. He started by carrying the xylophone himself and placing it next to the monochord, turning his back to me. Then he started to play on both instruments at the same time thus creating a rhythmical sound background. He swayed his body from side to side while sitting on the floor, for I work on the floor with children at the clinic. He started to invent songs or rather a sort of talking blues that could last up to twenty minutes. While at the beginning of a session there still might be some fits of anger expressed on the drum, the anger vanished as soon as the ritual started.

Swaying the body like this is associated with the hara (*water*, rhythm, centre of gravity, male/female balance, anger). It brings a harmonising of left and right, a pleasant bodily sensation that leads to an improved contact with the abdomen. It was evident that Rabbit was letting himself sink into the experience of sound. Through these mechanisms the separation of 'intellect' and 'body' disappeared automatically. This is a classic example of a lucid trance, since he kept full awareness during his chanting. A colleague once told me when we were talking about the trance movements of Rabbit how she had been working with a young woman for the last ten years in psychotherapy and how that woman had discovered for herself the beneficial effects of this kind of rhythmical swaying. The swaying movements used to calm her and she experienced an integration of her feelings as well as having pleasurable bodily sensations, which probably was reminding her unconsciously of being rocked herself as a baby in her mother's womb when her mother was walking. She would do the rocking often when she was starting to feel anxiety. It is very likely that our culture has cut us off from numerous rituals and means of self-healing, not least with the help of music, chanting and dance.

Rabbit started to do his grieving for the two cats that he had lost recently. He needed to sing his song for the cats for several months. Then came the time when we had to include 'all the dead dogs'. Some weeks later his song included 'all the human beings' that had died. This became my task, while he insisted on singing the 'cat song' at the same time. He told me to sing the song for his three grandparents who had died over the years. We did all this with much heart and soul, singing our heads off, him beating the drum, rocking his body and me playing my guitar. I was aware of the fact that the death of one of the grandmothers, in fact a great grandmother, whom I had to sing for, had occurred when Rabbit was still in his mother's womb. Both his mother and the children's psychiatrist had suggested her death as a possible cause of Rabbit's troubles. His mother had been very close to her grandmother. Therefore it is likely that during the mourning period she had for some weeks turned her attention away from the child in her womb, in so doing leaving the child in an emotional void while at the same time he was feeling his mother's distress strongly. This kind of occurrence is known to be a likely cause for autism.

Singing with Rabbit in this way for many weeks I could not but think of healing rituals done in some shamanic cultures in order to free the soul of the dead person. I thought also of the German psychiatrist Bert Hellinger's works, where he recommends that his clients restore the dignity of persons who have been excluded from the family circle for years (Hellinger 2002). His work does have strong shamanic traits and is probably rooted in his experiences during many years of working in South Africa with the Zulu population.

There are musical instruments that help to create this trance background and so help people to make contact with their body and their emotions. Such instruments usually create a reliable sound envelope. Drum, gong, monochord, harmonic bed, deep singing bowls, guitar in open tuning and even claves will serve to do this. They can help to induce a lucid and healing trance.

Inspiration and visionary work

In my experience musicians, including amateurs of course, are sometimes able to open a 'spirit door' indisputably leading into other levels of consciousness, towards new horizons for an individual or a collective. More than once unexpected pieces of music or unknown musical traditions have catapulted me out of my hearing and thinking habits. When this happened I felt disoriented for a short while and afterwards I would very often find myself in new open spaces. Revealing new horizons and bringing forward new visions are an important function of art – or felt expression – and can show us ways out of a cul-de-sac.

We all have the potential to express ourselves spontaneously with feelings. Each one of us is thus able to take part in producing new visions and can contribute to a renewal in our smaller and larger circles. A gong, a singing bowl, a simple percussion instrument, our voice, our body in movement may give us access to the expression of a moment of eternity. Such is music's nature and we cannot escape it. It is my conviction that a shaman is simply someone who has learned to use and trust his right brain function to bring about harmonisation and healing in a wounded being. In so doing he is closely linked to the five elements system and the energies that are part of them, including what one may call nature spirits, the spirits of animals that often offer us their help and share their wisdom. A shaman respects them deeply and lets himself be guided by them.

It is not necessary to accept all the aspects of the many shamanic traditions which think that spirits are behind every illness and emotion. This belief may work very well in the context of their own cultures, but our cultures are different. When we let ourselves be invaded by other people's emotions it is very likely that unconsciously we are attracted to those particular emotions. In this situation it is within our capability and it is our responsibility to deal with our own vulnerability. We do not need to look deeper into the nature of these outside influences. We deal with them using controls already present within us. We can let ourselves be guided by the visionary art of an artist. However, I do believe that we might take artists off their pedestals, where our forbears placed them, and at the same

time recognise that everyone can be part of a visionary art and can participate in new ways of cultural and individual renewal and healing. We need
to reclaim the faculty of healing ourselves and healing our communities.
Projecting that role onto a few artists and paying them distorted amounts
for their work is, in my opinion, quite inappropriate and prevents many
people from expressing their potential.

Conclusion

In this book I have presented evidence to show that our musicality, the quality of our musical expression, is nothing other than a true reflection of our deepest inner self, of our psycho-energetic being. A person's musicality is his or her audible fingerprint. The qualitative observation required to detect this is helped by using metaphorically the five elements earth, water, fire, air and space. While reminding us of the five principles composing our universe, each element also appears in a great variety of forms in nature as well as within each one of us. Each detail observed leads us to a deeper understanding of who we are, of what life is.

Through working on musical expression we change. Through undergoing deep personal change our music changes. I have endeavoured to set out some guidelines here so that the various connections and associations involved in all this can be better understood. However, I must remind the reader that any system serves only as a stepping stone. Using the five elements system does not in itself offer simplistic answers, rather it gives us the opportunity to launch out into the unknown. This approach opens up our feeling side, our intuition, it is a doorway giving access to energy and the imperceptible, which is the true home of sound. It is an approach designed to respect the richness and magic in each being because it invites us to recognise the value of having two hemispheres in our brain, two sides within us. Accordingly, the inner and the outer, logic and intuition, material and spirit, feeling and expression, human beings and the planet and its elements may all be reconciled using this approach.

Recognising the quality of an element inside us helps us to respect it within us, in others and in nature. Music is the playground for experiencing it, playing around with it. The word 'harmony' is again filled with meaning *in music as in life*. It is hoped that this helps to reveal other avenues for people engaged in music education, music therapy, in artistic expression in the realms of folk art and inspirational art.

Each musical element, as small and insignificant as it may seem, opens a door revealing invisible but felt worlds, an Ariadne's thread guiding us to the depth of pure being. The neuro-musical thresholds are precise landmarks along that path. They help us to work playfully on meaningful tasks.

I have looked at the different roots of our musicality: innate, biological, cultural and those coming from sources beyond our understanding. Indeed, personal experience and my observations of people I have worked with seems to confirm that an important part of our musicality has its roots in past lives. This can be shown in intense and inexplicable affinities with specific musical instruments, with music from cultures distant in place and time.

Conversely, such instruments or musical cultures can show us the way to approach these unfamiliar spaces. We are living in a period where we are discovering, possibly even re-discovering, the effects of sound, the existence of energy fields, the real function of our brain, quantum physics, a grounded way to embrace the spiritual dimension and new ways of healing. At the same time we have tools to identify preconceived ideas and limiting beliefs and we can learn how to overcome them. Let us keep a certain humility for we are just at the beginning. But let us take up the challenge.

Dordogne, January 2005

Musical Instruments

Throughout the ages human beings have created musical instruments and more recently ways to record musical performances in order to bring forth the magic of sound first heard in the imagination and which the voice could not reproduce. Musical instruments assist musical inspiration. They give us *wings*, connect us to the air element, and allow us to express a vision or an inner, wordless story. In recent decades craftsmen and manufacturers in all corners of the world have marvellously supplied us with numerous instruments. Many new ones have been created.

Musical instruments are sources of sound and as such have an effect on the musician and on the audience. They can contribute to sound healing even though we only now start to understand their specific action on our energy fields. They can be powerful allies for the therapist and recipient when used with clear and respectful minds.

Here I present a number of instruments that anyone can use for improvisation. They allow the players to meet at the same level. I usually use instruments that are by themselves sound events. They do not need to be expensive, as ceramic flowerpots testify. Some supermarkets offer cheap instruments made all too often with a lot of plastic and having no real sound quality. These are certainly not conducive to improvisation. Synthesisers may be wonderful, but a reasonable amount of money must be paid if the 'plastic' sound is to be left behind. This is equally true for CD recordings of synthesiser music. A craftsman's skill of course contributes to an instrument's magic and not just to its audible aspect.

Drums

Gong drums, table drums

You can import double frame drums from the Himalayas (Nepal). They measure some 60–110cm in diameter. In Switzerland and Germany there are now a number of makers who specialise in the large table drum (single skin, on four legs) and gong drums (usually a double frame drum to be suspended) and build them up to 130cm size. The sound of these large drums is even richer. Frame drums brings us at one and the same time into contact with the male energy from above (heaven, universe) and the female, motherly energy from the earth. They have been used throughout the ages for bringing together 'Heaven' and 'Earth'. They have the great advantage of being able to be played softly, displaying low tones and lots of harmonic notes at the same time, varying greatly due to where you play on them, at the edges or towards the middle. They can be played with very soft mallets with a top made of leather or fabric, filled with cotton.

Ocean drums

Theses are double frame drums containing a multitude of tiny metal marbles, that roll from side to side when held in a near horizontal position, giving the impression of the sound of waves rolling onto a beach, water. New born babies hearing this sound seem to be reminded of the sound of the blood moving in their mother's aorta while they were in her womb. The ocean drum can calm them in an extraordinary way, if played softly.

Slat drum

This is actually more of a xylophone than a drum. It is a rectangular closed wooden box where different length cuts on one side have produced keys of different lengths and tone. Its cavity gives it a warm sound thus favouring contact with the water element. It is easy to play because it lacks an obvious tonal organisation and has relatively few notes. It is played either with soft mallets, evoking water and air or with harder ones evoking fire and earth, according to the quality of sound you want. It does not require the player to develop melodies. Schlagwerk produces a large slat drum (120cm long) on which a child can lie down (http://www.schlagwerk.de/).

Strings
Koto/Monochord

The monochord is an instrument created some twenty years ago in Germany and Switzerland. Unlike Pythagoras' monochord, hence its name, the modern monochord has on one side some twenty-eight strings tuned in unison. On the other side it often has a tampura with four strings (fundamental, octave, two fifths) together with a Japanese Koto with some twelve strings with moveable bridges. The steel strings are about 1.2m long. Children are fascinated by it because of the echo effect heard when they sing into one of the three sound holes on its long sides. This magical aspect of the monochord is due to the resonance of its many strings and has helped many times to prompt a child to sing. With this instrument we can explore different aspects of the voice, amongst others the sounds that animals make. I usually succeed in making a shy child roar like a lion.

The monochord side allows the player to establish a dronelike sound background for singing and other musical activities. This drone effect creates a relaxing, mothering sound. Its energetic effect may bring about a feeling of expansion. You can easily tune its koto side thanks to its individual moveable bridges and any musical mode or tuning system can be set up. You can modulate each note while playing by pressing down each string on the left side of its bridge.

Soundbed

This is a very interesting recent creation also produced in either southern Germany or in the German-speaking part of Switzerland. It is a purely therapeutic instrument, a kind of large monochord on which you can lie down. There are several models available, most of which are hollow tables acting as sound boards. Underneath the table board are some fifty strings tuned in unison or sometimes in fundamental and fifth. People working with them claim that each frequency has a specific healing quality, for example G sharp would be used for relieving physical pain. Healers often tune its A to 432 hertz. As with the monochord, when the soundbed is played with precision on its mathematical fractions $\frac{1}{2}$, $\frac{1}{3}$, $\frac{1}{4}$, $\frac{1}{5}$ for instance, and when played by someone with a good ear, a whole series of overtones can be produced. The *overtone* scale creates an elevating feeling. Our senses naturally follow the rising overtones. Both monochord and soundbed soothe the nervous system and sharpen our hearing and other senses, eliciting a strong movement into the element of space.

Guitar

Keeping in mind the desire to offer people musical instruments that need very little playing technique, a guitar can be used in *open tuning* (i.e. EAEABE or DADF#AD). There are many other open tunings. This allows someone to play without an elaborate left-hand technique, since a perfect chord sounds when striking the strings. You can use the instrument in the same way as a slide guitar by sliding along the strings with a hard object such as a claves. In this way I can play the guitar with one hand while my other hand is beating a drum and I can sing at the same time.

Accordingly I can generate the qualities of earth when playing a rhythmical base, water when playing in an ever changing flow, fire (think of the flamenco guitar) and air (especially when playing melodically or using chords).

Metallophones
Singing bowls

Two types of this instrument are most commonly found: the Tibetan/Nepalese bowl and the Japanese steel singing bowl. Their respective sounds are quite different. You can play them with your fingertips, felt mallets or may rub them along the edges with a wooden stick. They create a very pleasant sound envelope that can, for example, be used as drone background for singing. The sound produced by the bowl shape encourages your awareness to rest in an inner centre inside yourself. Being a bowl the sound has a female, receptive quality. When you move a sounding bowl along your body surface, you will hear clear differences in the reverberation of its overtones. These indicate different densities in your energy field. While moving up and down the central axis you would be able to detect energy blockages associated with chakra centres or the navel.

Tubular bells

Tubular bells have a twofold action. They make us feel our spine, our vertical axis, a male characteristic, as well as prompting an expansive movement. Their sound seems to expand so fast to the periphery of the room, that often we lose the sense of where the sound started. As with all these metallic percussion instruments, their sound stays in the room for a rather long time. I find that these instruments allow us to expand our mental aura, if used in the appropriate circumstances, element space. In order to follow such an expansion in our energy field with our feeling awareness as well as with our hearing sense, we would necessarily have to abandon certain limiting thoughts such as that our mental energy field cannot possibly expand. Being open-minded in this context means that we may be able to allow our mental framework or 'horizon' to enlarge. The expansion of our mental energy field can be very beneficial for our overall health and can help us to overcome some habits connected with worrying or fear.

Hang

'Hang' means 'hand' in the Bernese dialect spoken in parts of Switzerland. This instrument with its unique sound was invented by people in Bern after they had studied the Jamaican steel drum and Balinean gamelans for a while. The shape reminds us of an unidentified flying object and is manufactured by putting two flat metal bowls together. The upper half has some seven carefully tuned hollows. At the time of writing the manufacturer, PANArt, offers some forty-five differently tuned hangs, each one in a different musical mode or key. It is best played with bare hands and fingertips. The sound is beautiful and reminds one a lot of the steel drum. If you choose to use felt mallets you may want to use them very carefully, since too strong a beating would detune a note which has been tuned by a precision hammering of the hollow. Its belly shape places the hang in the water element zone (www.hang.ch).

Cymbals

Cymbals can be a very useful instrument to bring out someone's fire quality. This is particularly so for people with an oversensitive solar plexus area and they can practice on cymbals at their own pace. When played too loudly, you can give someone a fright because the sound will go straight into their solar plexus and hit their nervous system. Through playing the cymbals someone may learn to handle their solar plexus energy by starting to push it outwards when the sound hits them. Again, it is important not to force the pace when playing for someone else. An over-vulnerable solar plexus has its own story, sometimes containing very old traumas that need to be worked with gently. See my comments in Chapter 2, on the element fire.

Glockenspiel

Well-known metal cousin of the wooden xylophone. For a good sound check the resonators underneath.

Gongs

Gongs usually have a powerful sound. There are a number of different kinds of gongs differing largely in size and sound. A single large gong can by itself open up worlds of different sounds. When played with sensitivity you can use gongs very effectively for sound healing. As with many metal percussion instruments, gongs can produce beneficial effects when played for self healing by a person with an oversensitive solar plexus zone. I have recognised from live performances and recordings which gong performances are likely to catapult you into what one might call the underworld, into the dark abyss of the subconscious. If worked with thera-peutically this can have a beneficial effect for some people. Since a gong's sound can easily be overpowering and penetrating, however, one might well resist being exposed to an inexperienced, insecure musician with unresolved ego problems. Gongs have already been used for sound healing in the western world for some twenty-five years. It is very likely that in countries where gongs are traditional and have been used for centuries if not millenia, musician healers would have much more experience than we have in the west, for example in China, Bali, Indonesia and Thailand. Any of the five elements' qualities can be brought forth on a gong. The Swiss manufacturer Paiste has created a whole series of therapeutic gongs, including models for the five elements (www.paiste.com).

Small percussion

Gungroos

Indian dancers often tie a ribbon of small bells around their ankles or wrists, thus emphasising every foot and hand movement they make. I have found these ribbons to be very effective for children who love them. The bell sounds help them to get more awareness into their feet and through that to develop a better grounding. Many adults could benefit from them too for the same reason. Why not from time to time walk around at home with gungroos on your ankles?

Claves

A pair of short sticks made of hard wood, giving off a sharp, dry sound when hit on each other. It is a very awakening sound typical of the spring and wood energies spoken of in traditional Chinese medicine.

Rattles, marrakas, chakchas

Rattles of all kind make us perk up, they stimulate our nervous system.

Whirly

Australian instrument consisting of a flat, small, almond-shaped piece of wood attached to a string. When whirling through the air it gives off a low buzzing sound.

Rainstick

You can produce a very relaxing effect with the Mexican rainstick, especially by working near the neck, shoulders and back of someone who is seated. The rainstick is made of a length of large diameter bamboo. Inside is a spiral of toothpick-size sticks pointing inward and many seeds or pebbles. The sticks prevent the little seeds or pebbles from falling down all at once and so a rainlike sound and feeling is produced as the seeds or pebbles trickle from one end to the other (water).

Small ceremonial cymbals or bells

These usually come in pairs and are made in Nepal, India and Tibet. When hit together they produce a sharp, penetrating, metallic sound. They can be used for sound healing since you can produce a variety of sounds exactly at the spot where you want to influence someone's energy field, for instance above energy points. Their quality for sound healing largely depends on the blend of metals used in their manufacture and whether or not they were originally made to be a pair.

Tuned percussion

Xylophone, marimba and African balafon

Recently I have come across the marimba, a wooden xylophone ('xylo' actually means wood in Greek) with resonators underneath. This instrument can be played with soft mallets or hammers and produces a very female sound that seems to envelop you with its softness. It can bring about a feeling of being in a cave, a womb, or of being wrapped up safely by the dark night sky (see album *Natural* by Fred Vogl, on Oreade records, Holland).

If one is launching into non-melodic playing, a pentatonic xylophone or indeed the African balafon can do the job beautifully. Pentatonic music hardly ever sounds wrong. This allows everybody to play together more easily. The African balafon is normally much cheaper than any European xylophone of comparable size. Balafons are usually tuned pentatonically. There are some beautiful single bass notes you can buy for the European xylophone.

Flowerpots

They certainly are a very cheap percussion instrument, easy to play with and producing very beautiful earthy sounds if chosen carefully. Flowerpots belong to the group known as lithophones. They have the extraordinary quality of helping well-trained musicians and amateurs alike to improvise. You will seldom be able to get a properly tuned set, so players have to drop any preconceived idea of playing melodies and chords. All you are left with is a dialogue between the flowerpots and your feelings. To create an appropriate set you may have to go to several shops and garden centres, possibly with your tuning machine so as to avoid always bringing home the same few notes.

Boom whackers

Short tube of plastic that gives off a tone when slapped on your thigh. One can easily be made by cutting up a length of light plastic tube into different and exact lengths. In this way you can tune them. This is not always necessary, however. They are also fun when not tuned and certainly can be played by everyone.

Wind instruments

Wind instruments are usually too difficult for young children to play or for anyone who has not learned to handle them. Therefore I will name just a few here.

Overtone flute

This particular flute usually has no finger holes. Its single note can be varied through overblowing, that is blowing more or less strongly. Then you can hear the natural overtone scale. The overtone flute does not require any technique involving fingers. It can therefore be played by children and people with disabilities.

Didgeridoo

This instrument comes originally from the Aborigines in Australia. It used to be made of wood from the eucalyptus tree. Its playing requires a special circular breathing technique. You can use a simple cardboard tube to get similar results. With children you can initiate some funny whispering dialogues or create the sounds of imaginary monsters. When played properly, that is when the musician has got a good grounding himself, the didgeridoo can be a very good instrument for directing awareness to the earth element and for improving one's grounding.

Harmonic tube

This is a very cheap, coloured, flexible plastic tube with ripples. By swinging them through the air you get the harmonic scale and whistling tones.

Keyboards

Synthesiser

The synthesiser cannot really replace the above-mentioned acoustic instruments as far as their effects are concerned. It does offer a complementary range of sound possibilities, that do not necessarily exist as yet on acoustic instruments. Some of its more common sounds have the quality of a choir, a church organ or a string ensemble and can bring about relaxation and some expansion in our energy field, especially when it is played together with an acoustic instrument as described above.

For me sound is sound, whether it is of synthetic or acoustic origin is secondary. What matters much more is whether the sound is beautiful and what effect it has on us. There are a great many cheap synthesisers which have a very poor sound. Some more expensive ones though can be very useful. They can produce sounds no other instrument can and they can be played by 'non-musicians' when used just for their sounds. People with disabilities, children and musically untrained persons can be helped to play beautiful and spacious sound carpets, space and air, using a synthesiser. They widen our horizons and help us into an expanded awareness if we remain in touch with the movements created.

Piano

It is quite easy to use a piano as a beautiful source of sound without using an advanced playing technique. You simply need to press down the right pedal which will naturally bring out all the resonance and overtones of a piano. You need not play very many tones, air and space mainly, but you can of course also play *fiery*, *watery* or *earthy* qualities.

Qualitative Research

I found Dorit Amir's thoughts on the question very inspiring. In the past, she says, 'positivistic' research rested upon five major assumptions:

1.   There is only one reality that can be broken apart into pieces that can be studied independently.

2.   It is possible to separate the observer and the object being observed. On one side we have the one that 'knows', on the other the one that is the object of the study.

3.   What is being observed in the present will remain true in the future. The focus is on prediction, not on understanding.

4.   There are no effects without causes and no causes without effects.

5.   It is possible to do objective research, that is, without the observer's system of beliefs influencing the results. That is why the researcher attempts to operate within a framework of the 'controlled procedure'.

(Amir 1993)

Dorit Amir is, on the contrary, convinced that these criteria are not applicable, neither in general, nor in particular in music therapy. She suggests that they may be replaced by new parameters allowing a qualitative research:

1.   The researcher is the key instrument. While researching, collecting and analysing information, the music therapist draws on his intuition, his feelings, his thoughts, in order to analyse this information and to understand its meaning.

2.   Qualitative research is based on descriptions, that is, on verbal language (even though drawings, audio and video recordings may be used).

3.   Qualitative researchers are concerned with the process rather than with the product.

4.   The analysis starts right from the beginning of data collection by organising the data and constantly constructing a picture which takes shape while its parts are being collected and examined. This process can be compared to a musical improvisation where we operate mainly within the field of the 'unknown'. We start by using several elements such as sounds, rhythms, dynamics and timbre while the improvisation

is under way. One is organising the elements and constantly constructing a sound-scape which takes shape while its parts are being collected and examined.

5.   There is a constant concern to capture the person's own way of interpreting significance as accurately as possible. The question is asked: what is the meaning of the experience for music-therapy clients as well as for music therapists.

(Amir 1993)

This is leading to the creation of a list of moments felt as being essential to the participants:

a)   *Moments of awareness and insight*, in which a sudden awareness is accompanied by a new meaning and occurred intuitively.

b)   *Moments of acceptance*, where the client accepts himself or integrates a part of himself in a manner unlike any before.

c)   *Moments of freedom*, that inlcude feelings of expansion and relief, resulting from a release of tension and letting go.

d)   *Moments of wholeness and integration*, in which the client experienced a feeling of being at one with themselves, accompanied by a feeling of peacefulness.

e)   *Moments of completion and accomplishment*, where the therapist feels that his efforts and explorations are bearing fruit and the client feels proud and has a sense of achievement in his music-making.

f)   *Moments of beauty and inspiration*, where the therapist feels inspired by the beauty, the courage and the authenticity of the client. Also, the client experiences her own inner beauty and a connection to the beauty that surrounds her.

g)   *Moments of spirituality*, where the client and the therapist feel connected to God, connected to his or her own soul and have some kind of mystical and sacred experience.

h)   *Moments of intimacy with self*, during which client and therapist reach a new, deeper level of intimacy with themselves physically, emotionally and spirtually.

i)   *Moments of ecstasy and joy*, in which therapist and client experience excitement, delight, joy and exhilaration during their musical journey.

j)   *Moments of anger, fear and pain*, where the client gets in touch with difficult feelings and emotions and expresses them either musically or verbally.

k) *Moments of surprise*, in which client and therapist are surprised by the quality and the intensity of their own experience or their client's experience.

l) *Moments of inner transformation*, when clients experience a powerful change that deeply affects their lives. The change is accompanied with a tremendous joy and excitement.

Appendix 3

Exercise for Centring Oneself

1. Contact an area of a square-type shape with its corners at the solar plexus, the spleen, liver and navel. Breathe into that square and feel this area.

2. Contact the focus area above the head (see Figure 1.1, which depicts the energy fields).

3. Feel well grounded in your feet and legs, feel your toes moving, establish as much concrete feeling as possible in each part.

4. Bring your awareness to your heart chakra and let a feeling of softness spread out from there into the space in front of you.

This exercise is combining different levels:

- the solar plexus area with its vulnerability to emotions

- the contact to the vertical energy of universal or spiritual intelligence, which comes to us from above our heads. This contact can also happen using the individuality point, but the focus position can often be a hindrance that needs to be worked with separately (the reason being that the edges of the focus position can hold on to emotional energy, which is linked to possible conflictual thought patterns concerning one's own spiritual beliefs)

- the important contact to the earth, which helps to ground spiritual energy and thoughts and makes that 'good intention' become useful

- the heart chakra, which brings the opportunity to gradually integrate these different levels.

This is a lasting process and takes patience as well as the intelligence of the heart. It allows for the therapist to combine intuitive, spiritual guidance, autonomy, practical grounding and compassion. Without these three dimensions in their work, therapists may experience a burn out or be caught in emotional unclarities. Strengthening these different levels allows one to stay clear, independent and inspired – independent, for example, from the restrictive thought structures of the client and other participants. This centring exercise is somewhat a concentrate of what needs to be included and worked with in personal development. We are working with a whole set of exercises, which help to strengthen grounding, intuition and the expression from the heart.

Geneviève Haag's Assessment Scheme for Autistic Children

Children's psychiatrist and psychoanalyst Dr Geneviève Haag has published in *Psychatrie de l'enfant* a scheme for the clinical assessment of evolutionary steps taken in the treatment of a child's autism. The group of specialists comprising psychoanalysts, psychiatrists, children's psychiatrists, neuropsychiatrists and psychologists who worked out this scheme included participants with some twenty years' experience. Geneviève Haag emphasises that human evolution rarely happens harmoniously. There will always be some aspects of development lagging behind others. A child may very well be proficient in one aspect, for example expressing his emotions, while at the same time showing no signs of evolution in spoken language. Fortunately these discrepancies are very often only temporary.

This assessment scheme is excellent and very detailed. It is, though, centred on autism experienced by young children. Many of the characteristics found in it are therefore very basic. Even though I have now been working for more than seven years with autistic children or rather with children within the autistic spectrum, I still feel that I lack experience concerning neuro-musical thresholds that would be relevant specifically for the evolutionary phases in autistic spectrum disorders. My observations seem for the moment to be more valid for children in post-autistic phases or for children, adolescents and adults who are not within the autistic spectrum. I shall therefore report here only Haag's observations that have a parallel with my neuro-musical thresholds (all references to the five elements are mine).

The research group directed by Geneviève Haag underlines the importance of following observable phases in the evolution of children's autism:

- the capacity to imagine oneself in another person's position, thinking or feeling what she might be thinking or feeling (theory of mind)

- expressing emotions towards others (water and fire)

- the importance of *tantrums* (water and fire)

- the look in his eyes: absent, escaping, piercing or sticking to you without penetrating* (fire)

- language: non-existent or echoing* (space)

- graphism: often non-existent*
- difficulties in picturing one's own body: states of hyper or hypotonicity*
- exploration of space and objects while using unisensorial stereotypes*
- grasping structure of time
- unidimensional time space where the child is lost/immersed in an ecstatic clinging on to a unique sensorial modality*
- circular time: importance of rigidly adhered-to rituals, looking for stable and non-changing components, repetitiveness* (earth)
- reaction to physical pain: non-existent or weak* (water)
- immune system conditions: strong resistance to infections*
- aggressive manifestations* (water).

*   Signs as manifested in the most severe autistic state.

Levels of Experience

1. a) *Physical* sensations: pain, tingling, heat, cold, heaviness, pressure, attraction to a particular place in body. The physical body and the etheric being a 'radar' of what takes place on other levels, these sensations can also be reflections from levels 2–11.

   b) *External* involuntary movements: of a hand, a leg, head, face, mouth, etc.

   c) *Internal* movements: intestines, sighs, salivary production, tears, changes in rhythm of breathing.

2. Observations on *etheric level* and subconscious memory: this information can come from levels 3–11.

   a) *Sensation of energy flow* travelling throughout the entire body, feeling in or around an energy centre, a psychic stream, feeling one body side is larger than the other, etc.

   b) *Hearing* experiences: internal dialogues with (a part of) ourselves or people from the past, present or imaginary, animals, objects; sounds, noises, music.

   c) *Visual* experiences: symbolic or archetypal imagery such as a dark cavern, tunnel, thick forest, thorn bushes, falling into a void, fire, fairy-tale or film figures, sorcerers, wise women, etc. colours, forms, movements, scenery, landscapes, animals, element (earth, water, fire, air), absence of sensations or emotions or contrary; visual memories or flashes of colour, etc.

   d) *Other senses:* smelling, taste, touch.

   e) *Resistance* to this information and tendency to escape (denial) from the physical/etheric sensations into

   - daydreaming, sleepiness, forgetting the experience, feeling of density without any possibility of penetration when 'drawing' a line on the skin's surface

   - emotional thoughts (doubt, worry, etc. see level 3)

   - physical activity like scratching, moving around, wanting to go to 'the fridge' and eat something.

3.   *Emotional* experience: anger, pain, impatience, fear, blockage and mental paralysis, jealousy, etc. Also unpleasant sensations like feeling imprisoned, 'cannot escape', being followed, 'cannot climb any higher', etc. Five hindrances or resistances: doubt, sleepiness, lack of concentration, impatience, irritation

4.   *Feelings* of joy, compassion, serenity, calmness, sense of unity with everything, well-being, etc.

5.   *Lower mental*: influenced by underlying emotions like worrying, solving daily problems, repetitive and vicious circles – can be accompanied by body tensions (neck, jaw, pit of stomach, weight on chest, etc.)

6.   *Upper mental*: without the interference of emotions; clarity of mind, symbols, geometric shapes, bright and clean colours, space, peace, intuitions

7.   *Causal*: memories of scenes from past lives, karmic links, sense of underlying deep causes

8.   *Soul level*: sense of our own qualities, aspirations, sense of purpose of our life

9.   *Spiritual* experience: being attracted by a light, sense of a spiritual being (angel, virgin, priest, wise beings), being in a cathedral, feeling the beneficial presence of a guide, etc. experience of well-being and expansion, of unity, contentment, calm; absence of thought and emotions

10.   Experiencing *energy*: unusual behaviour or transformation of the elements, visions, inexplicable, unknown or unexpected sensations or phenomena

11.   Experiencing the *unknown*, pure awareness, beyond words and thoughts: origin of impulses, absence of experience and sensations; unable to 'bring back' anything concrete at first other than a feeling of a presence or of having experienced something.

Music Therapy Evaluation Chart

	Absent	Little	Normal	Frequent	Exaggerated
General observations					
Visual contact with therapist	☐	☐	☐	☐	☐
Feeling contact with therapist	☐	☐	☐	☐	☐
Physical contact with therapist	☐	☐	☐	☐	☐
Manages to copy	☐	☐	☐	☐	☐
Learns 'with delay'	☐	☐	☐	☐	☐
Is interested in new instruments	☐	☐	☐	☐	☐
Switches from instrument to instrument if left to do so	☐	☐	☐	☐	☐
Uses instruments as non-musical objects	☐	☐	☐	☐	☐
Stereotypical behaviour:	☐	☐	☐	☐	☐
Has got the sense of the 'do re mi'	☐	☐	☐	☐	☐
Can memorise bits of melodies	☐	☐	☐	☐	☐
Is creative and inventive on non-musical level	☐	☐	☐	☐	☐
Uses his imagination in music	☐	☐	☐	☐	☐
Expresses emotions in music	☐	☐	☐	☐	☐
Helps clearing space at the end	☐	☐	☐	☐	☐
Singing and language					
Sings or hums	☐	☐	☐	☐	☐
Sings non-verbal sounds	☐	☐	☐	☐	☐
Understands what I say	☐	☐	☐	☐	☐
Speaks sentences with a minimum of five words	☐	☐	☐	☐	☐
Verbal communication with therapist	☐	☐	☐	☐	☐

	Absent	Little	Normal	Frequent	Exaggerated

Body

	Absent	Little	Normal	Frequent	Exaggerated
Dances alone (water)	☐	☐	☐	☐	☐
Dances with others (water)	☐	☐	☐	☐	☐
Dances rhythms (water)	☐	☐	☐	☐	☐
Fully uses his left side	☐	☐	☐	☐	☐
Fully uses his right side	☐	☐	☐	☐	☐

Quality of expression

EARTH

	Absent	Little	Normal	Frequent	Exaggerated
Self assurance, stable base	☐	☐	☐	☐	☐
Good contact with legs and feet	☐	☐	☐	☐	☐
Can concentrate	☐	☐	☐	☐	☐
Can keep a rhythmical pulse	☐	☐	☐	☐	☐
Can play on one instrument for a minimum of five minutes	☐	☐	☐	☐	☐

WATER

	Absent	Little	Normal	Frequent	Exaggerated
Has got vitality	☐	☐	☐	☐	☐
Access to creativity	☐	☐	☐	☐	☐
Fluent changes from one musical idea to next	☐	☐	☐	☐	☐
Is creative and inventive on musical level	☐	☐	☐	☐	☐
Good body contact (especially belly)	☐	☐	☐	☐	☐
Keeps on his own a complex rhythm for a minimum of thirty seconds	☐	☐	☐	☐	☐
Creates 'complex' rhythms (e.g. waltz)	☐	☐	☐	☐	☐
Violent and uncontrolled movements	☐	☐	☐	☐	☐
Takes care of instruments	☐	☐	☐	☐	☐
Hammers too strongly on instruments	☐	☐	☐	☐	☐

FIRE

	Absent	Little	Normal	Frequent	Exaggerated
Afraid of certain sounds	☐	☐	☐	☐	☐
Has got fire, tonus	☐	☐	☐	☐	☐
Expresses intensity in playing music	☐	☐	☐	☐	☐
Has got warmth in his/her expression	☐	☐	☐	☐	☐
Tendency to overly control session	☐	☐	☐	☐	☐

	Absent	Little	Normal	Frequent	Exaggerated
AIR					
Has got lightness, 'wings', joy	☐	☐	☐	☐	☐
Is interested and sensitive to sounds	☐	☐	☐	☐	☐
Melodic sensitivity and organisation	☐	☐	☐	☐	☐
Harmonic sensitivity	☐	☐	☐	☐	☐
Sense of beauty	☐	☐	☐	☐	☐
Depressive withdrawals	☐	☐	☐	☐	☐
Improvises with feeling	☐	☐	☐	☐	☐
Expresses with arms and hands while dancing	☐	☐	☐	☐	☐
SPACE					
There is space in his/her music	☐	☐	☐	☐	☐
Can listen to and comment on what others play	☐	☐	☐	☐	☐
Capable of musical dialogue with somebody	☐	☐	☐	☐	☐
Spontaneous use of voice	☐	☐	☐	☐	☐
Use of instruments					
Drum (mainly earth, water, fire)	☐	☐	☐	☐	☐
Monochord	☐	☐	☐	☐	☐
Small percussion	☐	☐	☐	☐	☐
Rainstick (water)	☐	☐	☐	☐	☐
Flute sound (air)	☐	☐	☐	☐	☐
Covers two holes	☐	☐	☐	☐	☐
Flowerpots	☐	☐	☐	☐	☐
Xylophone	☐	☐	☐	☐	☐
Cymbal (fire)	☐	☐	☐	☐	☐
Singing bowl (space)	☐	☐	☐	☐	☐

Dates and colours of ratings:

Major thresholds are printed in italics

Improvisation Techniques in Music Therapy

★ Asterisks denote material added by Daniel Perret.

Techniques of empathy	
Imitation	Echoing or reproducing a client's response, after the response has been completed
Synchronisation	Doing what the client is doing at the same time
Incorporating	Using a musical motif or behaviour of the client as a theme for one's own improvising or composing, and elaborating it
Pacing	Matching the client's energy level (i.e., intensity and speed)
Reflecting	Matching the moods, attitudes, and feelings exhibited by the client
Exaggerating	Bringing out something that is distinctive or unique about the client's response or behaviour by amplifying it
Sounding presence★	Cover/observe the client with out his/her awareness and watch peripherally, while we continue to play or hum a non-directive music, as if only playing for ourselves
Active listening★	Listening and once in a while describing verbally the client's music
Humour★	Exaggerate an element of the client's play or place it in another context, in order to make the client laugh, in order to help him feel more at ease and confident

Structuring techniques	
Rhythmic grounding	Keeping a basic beat or providing a rhythmic foundation for the client's improvisation
Tonal centring	Providing a tonal centre, scale, or harmonic ground as a base for the client's improvision (★e.g. 3 repeating chords, see also pentatonic scales)
Shaping	Helping the client define the length of a phrase and give it an expressive shape
Concentrate★	Help client to concentrate better on an instrument, to balance dispersion and loss of concentration (strengthen element earth)
Ritual★	Introduce beginning and ending rituals, to further feeling of security

Techniques of intimacy

Sharing instrument	Using the same instrument as the client, or playing it co-operatively
Giving	Presenting the client with a gift, such as a musical performance, instrument, or a stone* etc.
Boding	Developing a short piece or song based on the client's responses and using it as a theme for the relationship, *e.g. as a beginning ritual
Soliloquies	Improvising a song as if talking to oneself about the client

Elicitation techniques

Repeating	Reiterating the same rhythm, melody, lyric, movement patterns, etc., either continuously or intermittently
Modelling	Presenting or demonstrating something for the client to imitate or emulate
Making Spaces	Leaving spaces within the structure of one's own improvisation for the client to interject
Interjecting	Waiting for a space in the client's music to fill in the gap
Extending	Adding something to the end of the client's response to supplement it
Completing	Answering or completing the client's musical question or antecedent phrase

Redirecting techniques

Introducing change*	Initiating new thematic material (e.g., rhythms, melodies, lyrics, *nature element, *instrument) and taking the improvisation in a different direction
Playing techniques*	Show new techniques of playing or new way of making sounds with an instrument
Differentiating	Improvising simultaneous music that is separate, distinct and independent from the client's music, yet compatible with it
Modulating	Changing the metre or key, *scale or mode of the ongoing improvisation with the client
Intensifying	Increasing the dynamics, tempo, rhythmic tension, and/or melodic tension
Calming	Reducing or controlling the dynamics, tempo, rhythmic and/or melodic tension
Intervening	Interrupting, de-stabilising, or redirecting fixations, preservations, or stereotypes of the client
Reacting	After an improvisation or playback, asking the client what he or she liked or disliked about it
Analogising	After an improvisation or playback, asking the client to cite a situation in life that is analogous to the improvisation or experience
Intuition	Follow your intuition, analyse later!

Procedural techniques

Enabling	Instructing the client about improvising or otherwise assisting him/her
Shifting	Changing from one modality and/or medium of expression to another
Pausing	Having the client make 'rests' at various junctures in the improvisation *and make him e.g. breathe deeply into the belly
Receding	Taking a less active or controlling role and allowing the client to direct the experience
Experimenting	Providing a structure or idea to guide the client's improvisation and having him/her experiment with it
Conducting	Directing a musical improvisation through gestures or signs
Rehearsing	Having the client practice an improvisation *or parts of it
Performing	Having the client re-do an improvisation after it has been rehearsed
Playing back	Having the client listen to or view a recording of his/her improvisation
Reporting	After an improvisation or playback, having the client report on his/her experience while improvising

Emotional exploration techniques

Musical 'holding'	As the client improvises, the therapist provides a musical background that resonates the client's feelings while containing them
Physical holding*	The therapist provides a physical support, e.g. through putting one hand on the lumber area of spine or putting an arm around client and maybe playing at the same time on the same instrument (with children)
Physical holding*	Expressing feelings that the client is having difficulty acknowledging or releasing fully
Doubling	Having the client improvise opposite qualities or feelings (*see which of the five elements are missing in their expression; therapist can also play them himself if necessary)
Contrasting	Having the client find various ways within an improvisation to get from one quality or feeling to its opposite
Making transitions	Having the client find various ways within an improvisation to get from one quality or feeling to its opposite
Integrating	Introducing contrasting elements into the improvisation, then combining, balancing or making them compatible (*see again, the five elements)

Emotional exploration techniques cont.

Relaxation*	In accordance with the client's possibilities, make him/her aware while playing of belly breathing, relaxing shoulders, neck, jaw, face, legs, back, etc.
Sequencing	Helping the client to put things in sequential order (e.g., sections of an improvisation, events of a story, or autobiographical information)
Splitting	Improvising with the client two conflicting aspects of the client's self
Transferring	Improvising duets with the client that explore significant relationships in his/her life
Role-taking	Swapping various roles with the client while improvising
Anchoring	Associating a significant experience in therapy with something that will enable the client to recall it easily, or recasting the experience in a modality, medium or form that will externalise or consolidate it
Catharsis*	Encourage client to beat a drum with bare hands and use voice simultaneously. Use body and arms in order to exaggerate a musical expression (e.g. imitate thunder, lion's roar)
Body music*	Use parts of own body to produce sounds, chest, cheeks, thighs, hands, skull, fingers for example

Referential techniques

Pairing	The therapist improvises different musical motifs to selected client responses, and then plays the motif every time the client emits the response
Symbolising	Having the client use something musical (e.g., instrument, motif) to stand for or represent something else (e.g., event or person)
Recollecting	Having the client recall or imagine sounds that accompany a particular situation or event, and reproduce them
Free associating	Having the client say whatever comes to mind upon listening to an improvisation, including imagery, memories or associations
Projecting	Having the client improvise music that depicts a real situation, feeling, event, relationship, etc.
Fantasising	Having the client improvise music to a fantasy, story, myth, or dream, *body part, colour
Story-telling	Improvising music and stimulating the client to make up a story
Animals*	Express musically or vocally an animal and associated emotion

Discussion techniques	
Connecting	Verbalising or asking the client how various aspects of the client's experiences or expressions relate to one another
Probing	Asking questions or making statements to elicit information from the client
Clarifying	Getting the client to elaborate on, clarify, or verify information that has already been offered
Summarising	Verbally recapitulating events in therapy and stating them concisely, or reviewing the client's experiences or responses during a particular phase of therapy or life situation
Feedback	Verbalising how the client might appear, sound or feel to another person
Interpreting	Offering possible explanations for the client's experiences
Metaprocessing	Having the client switch to a level of consciousness that enables him/her to observe and react to what he or she is doing or feeling
Reinforcing	Rewarding the client or withdrawing reinforcement according to the client's behaviour
Confronting	Challenging the client by pointing out discrepancies or contradictions in his/her responses
Disclosing	Revealing something personal to the client, talking about oneself during a session
Projections*	Talk about one's own projections, feelings that come up through client's play, if appropriate

Adapted from Bruscia (1987).

References

Ainsworth, M.D.S., Blehar, M.C., Waters, E. and Wall, S. (1978) *Patterns of Attachment: A Psychological Study of the Strange Situation.* Hillsdale, NJ: Erlbaum.

Amir, D. (1993) 'Research in music therapy: Quantitative or qualitative?' *Nordic Journal of Music Therapy 2,* 2, 3–10.

Bertelsen, J. (1982) *Drømme, Chakrasymboler og Meditation.* Copenhagen: Borgen.

Biesenbender, V. (2001) *Plaidoyer Pour l'Improvisation in l'Apprentissage Instrumental.* Fondette: Editions Van de Velde.

Boadella, D. (1987) *Lifestreams: An Introduction to Biosynthesis.* London: Routledge and Kegan Paul.

Bruscia, K. (1987) *Improvisational models of music therapy.* Springfield, IL: Charles C. Thomas.

Damasio, A. (1994) *Descarte's Error: Emotion, Reason, and the Human Brain.* New York: Putnam.

Damasio, A. (1999) *The Feeling of What Happens.* New York: Harcourt Brace and Co.

Delion, P. (1997) *Séminaire sur l'Autisme.* Ramonville Saint-Agne: Editions Erès.

Diolosa, C. (2000) 'Die psychologie der fünf elemente.' In F.P. Redl (ed) *Die Welt der fünf Elemente.* Linz: Bacopa Verlag.

During, J. (1994) *Quelque Chose se Passe.* Lagrasse: Editions Verdier.

Feuerstein, G. (1990) *Encyclopedic Dictionary of Yoga.* London: Unwin paperbacks.

Fox, M. (2000) *Sins of the Spirit, Blessings of the Flesh.* Dublin: Gateway, Gill and Macmillan Ltd.

Gamborg, H. (1998) *Das Wesentliche ist Unsichtbar.* Reinbeck bei Hamburg: RoRoRo Sachbuch.

Gardner, H. (1994) *The Arts and Human Development.* New York: BasicBooks.

Gilles, E. (1993) 'Abusive head injury in children: A review.' *Western State University Law Review 20,* 335–378.

Glaser, D. (2000) 'Child abuse and neglect and the brain: A review.' *Journal of Child Psychology and Psychiatry 41,* 1, 97–116, Cambridge University Press.

Greenspan, S. (1997) *The Growth of the Mind: And the Endangered Origins of Intelligence.* Reading, MA: Addison Wesley.

Haag, G. (1998) 'Réflexions sur une forme de symbolisation primaire in la constitution du Moi corporel et les représentations spatiales, géométriques et architecturales corollaires.' In B. Chouvrier (ed) *Matières à Symbolisation.* Lausanne: Delachaux et Niestlé.

Hellinger, B. (2002) *Les Fondements de l'Amour in le Couple et la Famille.* Barret-sur-Méouge: Souffle d'Or.

Husson, A. (1973) *Huang Di Nei Jing Su Wen.* Paris: Association Scientifique des Médecins Acupuncteurs de France.

Irwin, E. (1988) *Working with the Elements.* Based on the teachings of Dharma Arya Akong Rinpoche. Edinburgh: Tara, Rokpa Trust.

John, Bina A. (2003) *Music in Early Childhood and Consciousness: A Philosophical Analysis of Intersections.* Doctoral dissertation, University of Toronto. Paper presented at RIME conference, Exeter.

Kenny, C.B. (1996) 'The Dilemma of Uniqueness: An essay on Consciousness and Qualities. *Nordic Journal of Music Therapy 5,* 2, 87–96.

Lehtonen, K. (1994) 'Is music an archaic form of thinking?' *Nordic Journal of Music Therapy 3,* 1, 3–12.

Malloch, S. (1999) 'Mothers and infants and communicative musicality.' In *Rhythms, Musical Narrative, and the Origins of Human Communication. Musicae Scientiae, Special Issue, 1999–2000,* 29–57. Liège: European Society for the Cognitive Sciences of Music.

Oldfield, A. (2000) 'Music therapy as a contribution to the diagnosis made by the staff team in child and family psychiatry.' In T. Wigram (ed) *Assessment and Evaluation in the Arts Therapies.* Radlett: Harper House Publications.

Perret, D. (1997) *Les Effets Subtils de la Musique – Une Approche par le Ressentis. Barret-sur-Méouge: Editions du Souffle d'Or.* (Exists in English as yet unpublished manuscript.)

Perret, D. (2001) 'Die "5 Elemente" in der Musiktherapie.' *Informationsblatt des Schweizerischen Fachverbandes für Musiktherapie SFMT 37,* 6–11; *38,* 13–17.

Perret, D. (2003) 'Die Wurzeln unserer Musikalität.' *Energie und Charakter.* Bühler (CH): Orgon Verlag.

Perret, D. (2004) 'Roots of musicality: On neuro-musical thresholds and new evidence for bridges between musical expression and "inner growth".' *Music Education Research 6,* 3. Basingstoke: Carfax Publishing, Taylor & Francis Group.

Perret, D. (2005) *Sound – Healing with the Five Elements.* Havelte (NL): Binkey Kok Publications.

Peukert, W.-E. (1976) *Paracelsus Werke,* Band III. Darmstadt: Wissenschaftliche Buchgesellschaft, p.462.

Platel, H., Price, C., Baron, J.-C., Wise, R., Lambert, J., Frackowiak, R., Lechevalier, B. and Eustache, F. (1997) 'The structural components of music perception: A functional anatomical study.' *Brain 120,* 229–243.

Quartz, S. and Sejnowski, T. (1997) 'The neural basis of cognitive development: A constructivist manifesto.' *Behavioral and Brain Sciences 20,* 537–596.

Reynolds, W. (1990) *Memories of a Music Maker.* Dublin: Comhaltas Ceoltóirí Eireann.

Rinpoche, K.T. (2002) 'The five Buddha families and the eight consciousnesses.' *Bodhi 6,* 1.

Rinpoche, S. (1992) *The Tibetan Book of Living and Dying.* London: Rider Random House.

Rinpoche, T.W. (2002) *Healing with Form, Energy and Light: The Five Elements in Tibetan Shamanism, Tantra, and Dzogchen.* Ithaca, NY: Snow Lion.

Roustang, F. (2000) *La Fin de la Plainte.* [An End to Complaining.] Paris: Editions Odile Jacob.

Saraswati, S. (2000) *Sure Ways to Self-Realisation.* Munger, Bihar, India: Bihar School of Yoga.

Satyasangananda, S. (2000) *Tattwa Shuddhi.* Munger, Bihar, India: Yoga Publication Trust.

Schopler, E., Reichler, R.J., Bashford, A., Lansing, M.D. and Marcus, L.M. (1994) *Profil Psycho-éducatif (PEP-R) Évaluation et Intervention Individualisée pour Enfants Autistes ou Présentant des Troubles du Développement.* Bruxelles: De Boeck-Wesmael.

Schore, A.N. (1994) *Affect Regulation and the Origin of the Self: The Neurobiology of Emotional Development.* Hillsdale, NJ: Lawrence Erlbaum.

Siegel, D.J. (1998) *The Developing Mind: Toward a Neurobiology of Interpersonal Experience.* New York: Guilford Press.

Tchendukua (2003) *Lettre d'information no. 8.* Vincennes: L'association Tchendukua.

Trevarthen, C. (2000a) 'Musicality and the Intrinsic Motive Pulse: Evidence from Human Psychobiology and Infant Communication.' *Musicae Scientae, Special Issue,* 155–215.

Trevarthen, C. (2000b) 'How music heals.' In T. Wigram and J. de Backer (ed) *Clinical Applications of Music Therapy in Developmental Disability, Paediatrics and Neurology.* London: Jessica Kingsley Publishers.

Trevarthen, C. (2002) 'Autism, sympathy of motives and music therapy.' *Enfance 1,* 86–99.

Trevarthen, C. (2003) 'Brain development, the human brain: Adapted for learning meanings from other people.' In Richard Gregory (ed) *The Oxford Companion to the Mind.* Oxford: Oxford University Press.

Trevarthen, C. and Aitken, K. (2001) 'Infant inter-subjectivity: Research, theory and clinical applications.' *Annual Research Review, Journal of Child Psychology and Psychiatry 42,* 1, 3–48.

Trevarthen, C. and Malloch, S. (2000) 'The dance of wellbeing: Defining the musical therapeutic effect.' *Nordic Journal of Music Therapy 9,* 2, 3–17.

Tustin, F. (1990) *Autism and Protection.* Paris: Seuil.

About the Author

Professional music therapist since 1990. Since 1996 Daniel Perret has been working as a music therapist at Brive hospital (Central France) in the day clinic for young autistic, psychotic and disharmonic children. He is the author of the books *Music – The Feeling Way* and *Sound Healing with the Five Elements*. His researches in music therapy have been published in *La Revue Française de Psychiatrie et de Psychologie Médicale*, the information bulletin of the Swiss Association for professional music therapy (ASMT), in the *Schweizerische Zeitschrift für Heilpädagogik*. Over the last 16 years he has been writing regularly on music and its effects for the Swiss quarterly magazine *Spuren*. Daniel Perret has a degree in Business Administration from the University of Zurich (1971). He has undergone an extensive training in transpersonal psychology and the effects of sound from 1979 to 1999 at the Psykisk Institut, Ringkøbing, Denmark. He is the director of the three-year training programme in Therapy and Music. He lives in Dordogne with his wife Marie Perret, an artist, psychotherapist and art therapist, who trains people in Art Synthesis. They have a son. As a musician he has been giving concerts since 1970 and has released 19 albums, eight of which are CDs.

With the group Blue Planet Sound, which he founded in 1998, his CDs are:

TranceLucid (with Irish percussionist Tommy Hayes and four other musicians)

Irish Ragas and Indian Airs (with Áine Uí Cheallaigh and three other musicians)

By Heart (with Irish singer Áine Uí Cheallaigh and Bríd Cranitch, keyboards)

Solo albums:

Celtic Soundscapes (Irish Low Whistle and other flutes)

Aulos (Schlesinger Scales on koto and keyboards)

Spirit of the Valley (Celtic Harp)

Yamalo – Dance with the Energy (music to the five Chinese 'elements')

Music for a Better World (with Friedrich Glorian)

Centre du vallon – courses, training programmes in Art Synthesis, Music and Energy, Therapy and Music
Marie and Daniel Perret, Le Vallon, Berboules, 24290 Sergeac, France
Vallonperret@wanadoo.fr   Tel. ++33 5 53 50 80 38

Subject index

Author index